William Jackson

The Four Ages

Together with essays on various subjects

William Jackson

The Four Ages
Together with essays on various subjects

ISBN/EAN: 9783744790512

Printed in Europe, USA, Canada, Australia, Japan

Cover: Foto ©ninafisch / pixelio.de

More available books at **www.hansebooks.com**

THE

FOUR AGES;

TOGETHER WITH

ESSAYS

ON

VARIOUS SUBJECTS.

———

BY

WILLIAM JACKSON,

Of EXETER.

———

LONDON:

PRINTED FOR CADELL AND DAVIES, IN THE STRAND.

M,DCC,XCVIII.

ADVERTISEMENT.

THE greatest part of these Essays should be considered as Sketches for a Periodical Paper, which was once intended for publication—they are, in consequence, upon familiar subjects, and treated as such—The Four-Ages, and other Pieces (easily distinguished) made no part of the above design; but though less proper for a Paper, they are more so for a Book, which may be considered as an addition to the THIRTY LETTERS already published by the same Author.

ERRATA.

ERRATA.

Page 148, line 1, for *professed* read *possessed.*
——— 174, ——— 7, for *faculty* read *facility.*
——— 299, ——— 17, after *into* read *the.*

The FOUR AGES.

———

THE Ancients, as Ovid elegantly
ſhews in his Metamorphoſis, held, that
the different ſtates of ſociety were aptly
expreſſed by being termed the Golden
Age, the Silver, the Brazen, and the
Iron—

> *Aurea* prima ſata eſt Ætas, &c.
> ————ſubiit *argentea* Proles
> Auro deterior, fulvo pretioſior Ære, &c.
> Tertia poſt illas ſuſcepit *abenea* Proles,
> Sævior ingeniis, &c.
> ————de duro eſt ultima *ferro.*

> METAM. LIB. I.

They conceived that the firſt ſtate of
man was ſuperior to all ſucceeding ſtates,
as gold is beyond other metals; that the

B ſecond

second Age had as much degenerated from the perfection of the first, as the value of silver is below gold; that the third was so far removed from primitive excellence, as to deserve the appellation of the Brazen-Age; and that the fourth, unhappily for us, is the last state of degeneracy, and deserves no better epithet than what the cheapest and most worthless metal afforded. We then live in the Iron-Age.

In compliance with a custom sanctioned by such early antiquity, I shall make use of the same terms, and call the different Ages by the names of the four metals, which, if not very elegant, are expressive enough of the meaning. But, in direct contradiction to the opinion of the ancients, and perhaps of the moderns, I shall, in treating this subject, invert the order, and endeavour to prove, that the first was the Iron-Age, and the last, when it shall please Heaven to send it, will

will be that of Gold—no Golden-Age
having yet exifted, except in the imagination of poets.

But to avoid being mifunderftood, it is
neceffary to premife, that the different
ftates of mankind do not depend upon
A. M. or A. U. C. or A. D.—for, in
the firft year of our æra, Italy was re-
fined, and England barbarous; and in
the eighteenth century, fome nations
have attained a point of perfection unknown to all which have preceded, while
others are ftill unenlightened and ignorant. It is not then from the age of the
world, but from the age of fociety, that
the dates in this effay are computed.

All works, whether of art or literature,
long fince produced, are ancient, as far
as time only is concerned. But if we
mean to diftinguifh between elegant and
barbarous antiquity, it is neceffary to
confider in what ftate of fociety the works

were

were produced. The want of this diftinction has been of great differvice to
the polite arts, and given a falfe direction to a good principle. At the revival
of the arts in Italy, architects, painters,
and fculptors ftudied the remains of ancient Rome as fpecimens of their art carried in an enlightened age to the height
of perfection. The Roman Antiquities
then are valuable, becaufe they are the
productions of artifts who poffeffed all
the knowledge of an advanced ftate of
fociety; but the Saxon and Gothic Antiquities, tho' juftly objects of curiofity,
and even of admiration, are ftill the remains of fociety in its infancy, and therefore barbarous and falfe.

Nothing is more common than finding
in nations widely feparated, a refem-
.blance of manners and cuftoms;* from
whence

* " Meet Highlanders near Montauban like
thofe in Scotland." YOUNG.

whence it is concluded, that they formerly have had some connection, and
that one has borrowed from the other;
as the Egyptians from the Chinese, or
the reverse; nay, the English from the
East Indians.* The custom of marking
the skin in figures was as much practised
by our anceftors in Britain, as by the
modern inhabitants of Otaheitee : † and
Robert

* " From Tartary the Hindoo Religion probably spread over the whole earth; there are signs of
it in every northern country, and in almoft every
fyftem of worfhip: in England it is obvious;
Stonehenge is evidently one of the Temples of
Boodh; and the arithmetic, the aftronomy, the
holidays, games, &c. ancient monuments, laws,
and even languages of the different nations, have
the ftrongeft marks of the fame original. The
worfhip of the fun and fire; human and animal facrifices, &c. have apparently once been univerfal."
ASIATIC RESEARCHES.

† To which may be added, the North-American
Indians, of whom Bartram fays, " their head,
neck, and breaft are painted with vermillion (colour) and fome of the warriors have the fkin of
the breaft, and mufcular parts of the body very

B 3   curioufly

Robert Drury's account of the practice of stealing cattle in Madagascar, differs in no circumstance from the Journal of a Focray, headed by Sir T. Carleton; as given in the Introduction to the Survey of the Lakes in the North of England.

It has puzzled historians to account for this connection, which in most instances is difficult, and in many, impossible. By adopting the idea, which it is partly the intention of this essay to establish, that man, in the same stage of society, is every where much alike;* and that ig-

norance

curiously inscribed, or adorned with hieroglyphick scrolls, flowers, figures of animals, &c. they prick the skin with a needle, and rubbing in a blueish tint it lasts for life."

* " The Egyptian, Hindoo, Moorish, and Gothic Architecture, instead of being copies of each other, are actually the same—the spontaneous produce of genius in different countries, the necessary effects of similar necessity and materials."

HODGES.

The

norance of the arts, or knowledge of them, marks the character of ancient and modern ſtates of nations—the difficulty vaniſhes.

A great reſemblance may be obſerved between ſome characters and adventures in the Arabian Tales, and ſome in the old

The following quotation is of more modern application. " It is highly probable that many ceorls and burgeſſes, who dwelt in or near the place where a wittenagemot was held, attended as *intereſted* ſpectators, and *intimated their ſatisfaction with its reſolves by ſhouts of applauſe*—omnique populo audiente et vidente aliorumque fidelium infinita multitudo qui omnes laudaverunt."

HARDY.

This is a juſt picture of the National Convention of France, and evidently ſhews, that by reverting to firſt principles, they have alſo reverted to barbariſm.

The Muſcogulges (a ſavage nation in North-America) have the game of hurling, ſo very like that of Cornwall, that the deſcription of one would ſerve for the other.

B 4

old Provençal Romances. There is no reafon for fuppofing that the works of either reached the other. Imagine only that fociety was in the fame ftate in both countries, and it naturally accounts for a famenefs of character and incident.

The tumuli called, by the common people in the weftern counties, barrows, are to be found in every part of Europe, and even of Tartary. Before the art of building with ftone exifted, or when it coft more than early ages could afford, the moft natural monument, in any coun-try, over a man who deferved remem-brance, was a heap of earth. To this day, barrows are fhewn in Greece, as the tombs of Homer's heroes,

It would not be eafy to trace any con-nection between the modern Irifh and the ancient Greeks and Romans; yet, the former have, and the latter had, the fame cuftom of howling over the dead.

The

The lamentations over Hector's corpfe in Homer, and over Dido's in Virgil; which the latter calls Ululatus, fcarce differ from the Ulaloo of the Irifh. It is faid by a learned traveller, " that the Irifh are ftill in poffeffion of certain cuftoms utterly relinquifhed by the other nations of Europe"—if fo, then it proves that they are ftill in a ftate of fociety which is congenial to fuch manners and cuftoms, and that other nations have loft them becaufe they are advanced into another Age,

Let thefe few inftances fuffice to eftablifh my pofition; they might be much increafed if more were neceffary.

The firft of the four Ages then, is man in his favage ftate, wherever found, and at whatever period; the fecond is when he has made fome progrefs towards civilization; the third is the ftate in which we are at prefent; and the fourth is that

to

to which we are approaching, if no unfortunate event arrives to cut off our *golden* hopes. *

To

* There is no determinate point in which one Age ends, and another begins ; the former takes by degrees the colour and cast of that which is to succeed, and the latter Age for some time may preserve part of the barbarism and prejudices of the preceding. Thus some circumstances in the Iron and Brazen-Age may belong to either—the end, also, of the Brazen, and the beginning of the Silver Age, may intermix with each other.

Perhaps, the Silver-Age shewed some faint beginnings in England, during the reign of Queen Elizabeth—it continued to make a progress until the civil wars, when the times had quite the character of the Brazen-Age, or worse. Upon the restoration we advanced again, and have since been increasing in velocity towards perfection, like a comet as it approaches the sun. This image is rather too sublime for my purpose. The motion of a comet is regular and uninterrupted ; but there are many circumstances perpetually in the way of improvement, by which it is retarded partially, tho' it cannot be altogether obstructed. I have elsewhere touched on this subject.

To form a proper idea of man in his primitive ſtate, it is neceſſary to throw off all the refinements that the invention and cultivation of the arts and ſciences have beſtowed on ſociety, and ſhew what beings we are in a ſtate of nature.* And this is different according to the climate and productions of the country in which we live. Thus, in the Tropical Iſles, tho' the natural ſtate is ignorant and bar-

barous,

---

* If this were the ſtate of our firſt parents, it could not be a very deſirable one, according to the poet,

Quand la Nature étoit dans ſon enfance
Nos bons aïeux vivoient dans l'ignorance—
*　*　*　*　*
Mon cher Adam, mon gourmand, mon bon Pere,
Que faiſois-tu dans les Jardins d'Eden?
Travaillois-tu pour ce ſot genre humain?
Careſſois-tu Madame Eve ma Mere?
Avouez-moi que vous aviez tous deux
Les ongles longs, un peu noirs et craſſeux,
La chevelure aſſez mal ordonnèe,
Le teint bruni, la peau biſe et tannèe, &c.

VOLTAIRE.

barous, yet the people feem to be happy: but in Staten-land and Terra del fuego, ignorance and barbarifm take a favage caft, and the inhabitants have an appearance of wretchednefs and want, which is unknown in happier climates.

But there is even yet a lower ftate of human life—that of the *folitary* favage, (for fociety in its worft ftate is better than none)—a few fuch beings have been known to us: within this century a lad was caught in Germany, and a girl in France, both of whom had run wild from their infancy. Thefe are fcarce worthy of any rank even in the Iron-age, and were fome degrees below a domefticated dog or cat.

The characteriftics of the Iron-Age feem to be thefe:

Violence—

As there is no principle to reftrain the firft impulfe of defire, whether it be to

eat,

eat, or kill, or to attain any other purpofe, a man in this Age muſt naturally
ruſh on to the point propofed, regardlefs
of impediments or confequences.   If
food be in his reach, he eats voracioufly;
if the enemy be in his power, he gluts
his vengeance by every circumſtance of
cruelty.   The cuſtoms of the North-
American favages are well known, and
too horrid for quotation, I will therefore
give an inſtance from another people, of
that violence which is the prominent characteriſtic of favage life.   " The more
important the caufe that calls them to
arms, the more greedy they are of death.
Neither the bravery, nor the number of
their adverfaries can at all intimidate
them : it is then they fwear to *deſtroy the
fun.*   They difcharge this terrible oath
by cutting the throats of their wives and
children, burning all their poſſeſſions,
and ruſhing madly into the midſt of their
enemies !"   Said of the Koriacs by De
Leſſeps.

A

A want of great focieties—

The inhabitants even of a fmall ifland are feldom under one chief—their firft ftep towards the Brazen-Age, is the melting down of many little ftates to make a large one.

An ignorance of all the arts and fciences—

Except thofe which are immediately neceffary for ornamenting the perfon*— procuring food—covering—and weapons for each individual.

An abfence of all religious ideas—

Of

* People in this ftate of fociety confider ornament as of the firft confequence.—Nothing can fhew the efteem in which it is held more, than the great bodily pain they endure in order to be beautiful.—Boring of nofes, ears, lips, &c.—puncturing the fkin to make flourifhes on it, and other cuftoms of this fort, are more or lefs practifed by all unformed people in every country and climate.

Of courfe, no worfhip of a fuperior being, or belief of a future exiftence.†

Selfifhnefs—

As this quality is ftrongeft in the folitary favage, and is nearly extinguifhed in the laft ftate of fociety, we muft fuppofe it to be very powerful in the Iron-Age, and in fact we find it fo. Savages feek food, &c. for themfelves only, unlefs forced to procure it for their fuperiors :

few

---

† It has been faid, there are no people fo rude, but have fome religious worfhip—but this is not true—man in the Iron-Age, which we are now defcribing, has invariably been found untinctured with any principle of gratitude to the deity for bleffings received; of hope, for bleffings to come; or of fear, for laws tranfgreffed. When Warburton, in his Divine Legation of Mofes, afferted, that all nations worfhipped fomething or other, and believed in future rewards and punifhments; one of his adverfaries brought the Hottentots as an inftance to the contrary—both were right.—The affertion was taken from man in his fecond ftage of fociety; but the objection, from man in his favage ftate.

few inftances occur of their parting with any thing from a principle of kind-nefs.

A want of curiofity——

That is for fuch things as are *far* be-yond any to which they are accuftomed.—— Thus, they do not confider a fhip as an objeƈt of attention; but a canoe much larger, or more adorned than they have been ufed to fee, would attraƈt their notice.*

I have already remarked, that in the fame Age, one people may be civilized, and another, barbarous: to which muft be added, that thefe different ftates of fociety exift in the fame country at the fame time, according to the different fituations or employment of the inhabi-tants.

* Moft of thefe charaƈteriftics are taken from defcriptions of favage people, by the late voyagers, who found them in the fame ftate of fociety, tho' in different countries.

tants. Thus a mere ruftic in England, who never faw any other affemblage of houfes or people than the neighbouring village or church prefented, is as it were extinguifhed in the capital; but his curiofity would be excited, and highly gratified by a fair, or a cathedral church. In a fair are more people, more cattle, and a greater difplay of finery than he ufually meets with; but it is all of that kind for which his ideas are already prepared. The fame may be faid of the cathedral—he confiders it as his own village church upon a grander fcale. But an habitual exercife of the judgment is required to comprehend an idea, *greatly* fuperior to common exertion, as in the inftance of the fhip abovementioned: and it belongs to a cultivated ftate of the mind to admit an idea perfectly new.

Whenever it happens that a people in the Iron-Age have abated of perfonal violence, have made fome attempts, however

C

ever imperfect, towards art and science, that they entertain religious ideas, and are curious in observation and enquiries, they are then getting forward into the Brazen-Age.

We may consider the Brazen-Age as that state of society when people begin to refuse immediate gratifications for future convenience.—

Very few advances from the savage state are necessary for a Koriac, sometimes to feel the want of help from a wife whom he had killed in his fury—to find that if he had not gorged himself yesterday, he might have had something to eat to day. These sensations, often repeated, at last produce a restraint upon his inclination, and he finds that it is for his interest, sometimes to resist immediate gratification.

When a greater number of people are associated together than in the Iron-Age.—

If

If in the quarrels of individuals, repeated victory happen to the same person, he naturally becomes a chief—When
chiefs dispute, if one frequently gets the
better of others, he becomes master of
an extent of country; which, from the
same train of causes and effects upon a
larger scale, at last makes him a king;
—this is the origin of despotism, which
undoubtedly is the most natural and
ancient of all governments.*   If this
king,

* And despotism, sooner or later, produces liberty—Extraordinary acts of cruelty committed
by a weak Prince, give the first hint for shaking off
his authority—His subjects rebel and conquer.
They then make terms with their Prince, and
oblige him to govern upon principles dictated by
themselves, as in the case of King John; or resolve
to have no Prince, and so become a Republic, as
formerly in England, and latterly in France—And
this is the origin of all free governments. But as
in the avoiding of one extreme, we naturally run
into the other—A Republic, which succeeds to
despotism, is little better than no government at
all, by personal liberty being pushed to excess.

This

king, at his death, leave a fon of fufficient age and underftanding to continue
his father's confequence, he naturally
fucceeds; if not, the brother, or fome
other relative has a fair pretence to the
fucceffion—And this was the cafe in England during the Saxon Heptarchy, and is
fo even now with all Afiatic Governments, which ftrongly marks them to be
ftill in the Brazen-Age.

All private difputes between man and
man are carried on and terminated more

by

This gives an opportunity for fome one man of
abilities to take the lead, as in the inftance of
Cromwell. As defpotifm produces liberty, liberty
in its turn may revert to defpotifm, which was
nearly the cafe in the reign of James the fecond.
The people then perceive, that the beft way to
avoid the inconveniencies of either fyftem, is by
having a Stadtholder or Duke as in Holland and
Venice, a Prefident as in the United States, a Directory as in modern France, or by a limited Monarchy, fuch as now eftablifhed in England by the
Revolution of 1688, which, with all its faults, is
the moft perfect conftitution yet exifting.

by force than reafon. Bargains, promi-
fes, and even oaths themfelves are kept
or broken according to convenience.*

Cruelty—

Tho' not under the fame violent form
as in the Iron-Age, yet exifts in its full
force. K. John burns out the eyes of
Arthur; a practice that has ever obtained
in the defpotic Mahometan governments.
I fhall not ftain my paper with many
examples from the numberlefs inftances
which our hiftories furnifh: but fomething muft be produced to prove my affertion. Permit me then juft to mention
a circumftance in the death of the Duke
of York, (father of Edward the fourth)
when

* The intercourfe which our fettlements in
India have lately had with the native princes of
that country, affords many inftances of this characteriftic—Perhaps Tippoo Sultan's frequent breach
of promife and treaty, is more owing to the ftate
of fociety in which he lives, than to his having a
bad heart.

when Margaret and her affociates gave him " a clout dipp'd in the blood of pretty Rutland, to dry his eyes withal." And at leaft one hundred and fifty years later, after the Silver-Age had begun to dawn on us, when a bifhop with his own hand tortured a beautiful young woman for denying tranfubftantiation, or fome fuch reafonable caufe. Even in the reign of Charles the firft (fo long is this favage quality in wearing out) the fentences of the ftar-chamber breathe the cruelty, tho' not the ferocity of the moft barbarous Age. For writing a book, which at this time would fcarce be deemed offenfive, the fentence was (which I abridge from Rufhworth)—imprifonment for life—a fine of ten thoufand pounds— degraded—whipt—fet in the pillory— one ear cut off—one fide of the nofe flit —branded on the cheek—whipt and pil- loried again, and the other part of the fentence repeated. This unfortunate gentleman (adds my author) was well- known

known for his learning and abilities, &c.

Folly, cruelty, and fuperftition make up their religion and laws.—

The hiftorical part of all religions framed in this ftate of fociety, in which the actions of the deity are recorded, feems too abfurd for ferious obfervation —and the idea that we muft torment ourfelves in order to become acceptable to a being, whom we term the God of mercy, has occafioned too much mifery to be ridiculed. The whims of holy fuperftition are too numerous for the flighteft mention; many volumes might be filled with the nonfenfe which every country holds facred, from China round the Globe to America. I fhall not quote any well-known legend, but to avoid offence take an inftance from the religious code of Abyffinia. " Hagiuge-Magiuge are little people not fo big as bees or flies of Sennaar, that come in great

fwarms

fwarms out of the earth: two of their chiefs are to ride upon an afs, and every hair of that afs is to be a pipe, and every pipe is to play a different kind of mufic, and all that hear and follow them are carried to Hell." I do not extract this as being more abfurd than Afiatic or European belief, but there is a whimfical turn in it which makes it original as well as ridiculous. To this I will add a quotation from Chardin, upon a fubject partly religious and partly medical—It is a remedy for fterility. " The relations of the woman who is to be cured, lead her from her houfe to a particular mofque by a horfe's bridle, which they put upon her head over her veil. She carries in her hands a new broom and a new earthen pot full of nuts.* Thus equipped they

make

* Scattering of nuts was a cuftom at marriages in ancient Italy and Greece, and what more relates to the prefent purpofe, made part of the facrifice to Priapus. It is difficult to affign any other

reafon

make her mount to the top of the Minaret, and as fhe afcends fhe cracks upon
each ftep a nut, puts it in the pot, and
throws the fhell upon the ftairs. In defcending fhe fweeps the ftair-cafe, carries the pot and the broom into the choir
of the mofque, and puts the kernels of
the nuts in the corner of her veil, together with fome raifins. She then goes
towards her home and prefents, to fuch
men as fhe meets, that are agreeable to
her, a few of thefe nuts and raifins, de-
firing them to eat.* The Perfians firmly
believe that this cures fterility."

Some

reafon for this refemblance between fuch diftant
people, than that it begun when thefe nations were
in the fame ftate of fociety.

* This bufinefs feems very extraordinary to an
enlightened European. We think it ridiculous, and
feel all the folly of a fuperftitious ceremony when
the inftance is new, and wants the aid of cuftom to
eftablifh it. A Turkifh officer taken prifoner in
the late war between Ruffia and the Porte had this
article

Some fuperftitions only excite our pity;* but there are others which have cruelty connected with them, and produce more uneafy fenfations. The monaftic confinement—the abftinence and flagellations of the Papifts—and the voluntary torments endured by the Faquirs, have all their origin in the Brazen-Age; and, fanctified by cuftom, are continued

article in his journal. " To day I faw a proceffion in which a woman carried a child to the church—after faying fome prayers, the prieft fprinkled the child with water—this, they told me, made it a chriftian, and it had this great effect upon the child, that if it had died before the ceremony, it would have been tormented for ever, but if it were now to die, it would be eternally happy—fo great is the virtue of a few drops of water !"

* And fome excite our ridicule. " Laud, Archbifhop of Canterbury, in a fermon preached before the Parliament about the beginning of the reign of Charles the firft, affirms the power of prayer to be fo great, that though there be a conjunction or oppofition of Saturn or Mars, (as there was at that time, one of them) it would overcome the malignity of it."

AUBREY.

nued when the times are much too enlightened to admit of their firſt introduction.*

Folly, naſtineſs, and ſuperſtition, con-
ſtitute their art of phyſic—

The cauſe of diſorders is not attributed
to intemperance, or to any deviation
from natural rectitude, but to the ſhoot-
ing of ſtars, the appearance of comets,
to ſome old woman's evil eye, &c. and
their cure does not depend upon a rational treatment, but upon ſomething
done in the growing of the moon,‡ upon
verſes

* In May, 1789, a bill was brought into the
Houſe of Lords to repeal the ſuperſtitious laws of
Elizabeth and James the firſt, reſpecting penalties
for not going to church, &c.—the quotations from
theſe acts exhibit a true ſpecimen of the religion of
the Brazen-Age.

‡ " Not even a plant of medicinal uſe, but was
placed under the dominion of ſome planet, and muſt
neither be gathered nor applied, but with obſer-
vances that favored of the moſt abſurd ſuperſtition."

PULTENEY's SKETCHES of BOTANY.

verſes recited; or to certain words worn
about the neck, &c. and if medicine is
uſed, it is either ſomething very difficult
to be obtained, or ſomething too naſty
to be taken. M. Gmelin and his aſſo-
ciates who ſurveyed as philoſophers the
. Ruſſian dominions, ſpeaking of the inhabitants in one of the provinces, ſay " a
great number of their medicines, (like
thoſe of the old diſpenſatories in Europe)
are taken from the animal kingdom. Of
all their remedies of this ſort there is
none they hold in ſuch high eſtimation as
the gall of a creature called Dom, which
is a native of the Altais Mountains and of
Tibet. Human and bear's gall are ſcarcely
leſs precious. They think alſo that there
is great virtue in human fleſh and fat.
The fleſh of a ſerpent is eſteemed as a
ſpecific for bad eyes—that of a wolf for
a diſordered ſtomach—a wolf's tongue
for a ſore throat, &c."

" I

" I will give one inftance (fays Pulteney in his Sketches of Botany) from
Apuleius, of that credulity and fuperftition, which, fanctioned by antiquity, yet
prevailed in the adminiftration of remedies ; and exhibits a melancholy proof of
the wretched ftate of phyfic, which,
through fo many Ages, had not broken
the fhackles of Druidical magic and im-
pofition. As a cure for a difeafe called
by the French l'aiguillette nouèe, you
are directed to take *feven* ftalks of the
herb lions-foot, feparated from the roots ;
thefe are to be boiled in water in the
wane of the moon. The patient is to
be wafhed with this water, on the approach of night, ftanding before the
threfhold, on the outfide of his own
houfe ; and the perfon who performs this
office for the fick, is. alfo not to fail to
wafh himfelf. This done, the fick perfon is to be fumigated with the fmoke of
the herb Ariftolochia, and both perfons

are

are then to enter the houfe together, taking ftrict care not to look behind them while returning—after which, adds the author, the fick will become immediately well."

Touching for the king's evil perhaps would ftill have exifted had the Stuart family been upon the throne. Even in the prefent times people crowd about a dying malefactor to have their faces ftroaked. But the ftrongeft inftance of the fuperftition of the Brazen-Age protracted beyond its time, is animal magnetifm; the exiftence and virtue of which are believed by thoufands, who do not deferve the honour of living in the prefent ftate of fociety.

War and fuperftition furnifh the principal events of their hiftory.—

As the elegant arts, philofophy, ma‧ thematics, and all the train of fciences

do

do not exiſt in the Brazen-Age,* there is ſcarce any ſubject left for the writers which

---

* No doubt, architecture, ſculpture, painting, and muſic, exiſted; but ſo very imperfectly, as not to merit the appellation of *elegant* arts.

The buildings in this period of ſociety are as much inferior to thoſe of the preſent times, as ſuperior to the wretched huts of the Iron-Age; in all inſtances except where great exertions are made. In that caſe, the characteriſtic of violence (abated, but not extinguiſhed) produces effects unknown, and perhaps unattainable in more poliſhed times. The gothic cathedrals are proofs of this. From their ſize alone they acquire grandeur of effect, from the peculiarity of their ſtyle of building they are removed from all common-place ideas, and from both theſe cauſes inſpire devotion: they are ſtill an incongruous maſs of abſurdities, and truly belong to the times in which they were erected. But, if violence is more the character of the Iron-Age, why does it not produce ſuperior effects at that time? It does produce ſuch effects as are conſiſtent with the ſtate of the human mind at that period—ſuch as placing vaſt ſtones in circles, or ſuſpending and balanciñg them upon points, erecting pyramids, &c. but it wants ſcience for ſuch complicated works as churches, &c.

The

which fuch times produce, but that of war—diverfified by its being fometimes the

The fculpture and painting of the times bear an incorrect refemblance to the forms they would reprefent, and to atone for the want of truth and proportion, are elaborate in trifles.

The mufic, if we are to judge from what has reached us, is perfectly without melody and harmony, for furely an unmeaning fucceffion of notes and chords cannot be fo termed. Specimens of thefe arts are inconvenient to be given; but, perhaps the following is an example of what was confidered as elegant oratory at a later period—tho' the fpeaker was ftill in the Brazen-Age.

When Charles the firft arrived at York, in his expedition to Scotland, the Recorder addreffed him to this effect—" He begged his Majefty's pardon that they had caufed him (their bright and glorious fun) to ftand ftill in the city of York; a place now fo unlike itfelf; once an imperial city, where the Emperor Conftantius Chlorus lived and died, in whofe grave a burning lamp was found many centuries of years after: a place honoured with the birth of Conftantine the Great, and with the noble library of Egbert—and afterwards twice burned—and yet the births, lives, and deaths of emperors are not fo much for the honour of York, as that King

the private quarrels of individuals, and
fometimes an affair of a whole nation.
In either cafe the ftars, or fome fuperftitious application, determine the conducting of the bufinefs; and they rely lefs on
the valour of the combatants, than their
beginning the enterprize in a lucky moment. Burnet, in his account of the
Prince of Orange's landing at Torbay,
fays,

King Charles was once Duke of York, who had
given them a moft benign and liberal charter, and
maintains a lamp of juftice there, which burns more
clearly than that found in the grave of Chlorus,
and fhines into five feveral countries, by the light
whereof each fubject may fee his own right: that
the beams and lightnings of his Majefty's eminent
virtues did caft forcible reflections upon the eyes of
all men—That he had eftablifhed his throne upon
the two columns of piety and juftice. They offered him the beft of facrifices, their obedience,
not refembling thofe out of which the heart was
taken, and nothing of the head left but the tongue;
for their facrifice was that of their hearts, not of
their tongues."

RUSHWORTH.

D

fays—" The next day being the day in which the Prince was both born and married, he fancied if he could land that day, it would look aufpicious to the army, and animate the foldiers—but, we all, who confidered that the day following being gun-powder-treafon day, our landing that day might have a good effect on the minds of the Englifh nation, were better pleafed to fee that we could land no fooner."*

A fword bleffed, or enchanted, according as the hero is connected with a faint or a conjurer, renders its edge irrefiftible, except by armour that is alfo enchanted, and then the champion who has the moft powerful patron, is the conqueror.

Thefe

---

* Robert Drury, in his account of Madagafcar, informs us, that they were " juft about to begin an expedition, which was ftopped by a prieft becaufe it was in an unlucky time."—I do not know whether it was the fourth or fifth of November.

These circumstances still characterize many nations in Asia, who have not advanced beyond the Brazen-Age, and they equally belonged to the most polished people in Europe before they advanced into a state of refinement. France was recovered from the English by a virgin-warrior, whose arms were for a time irresistible, and her body invulnerable. It was very barbarous, say the French historians, to burn this damsel—it was so, but it was the barbarity of the times, not of the English.

Shakespeare faithfully copied the Scottish Historians in Macbeth's Adventure with the three Witches. The Weird Sisters held their ground long—I am not sure whether even at this time they have absolutely lost their existence. What the legislature thought in the times of James the first, is clear by the Act against Witchcraft—there is nothing surprising in this —it is but one circumstance out of many

D 2   which

which mark the fuperftition of the age.
But by what means can we poffibly account for the witches confeffing themfelves really guilty of the crime for which
they were to fuffer? A crime which never exifted, and a confeffion which muft
enfure immediate execution!*

With

---

* There was an inftance of this fo late as the
year 1697, when feven people were executed, who
declared themfelves guilty, and that their punifhment was juft. To add to the wonder, I will here
fubjoin the reply of one of the council to another,
who wanted to acquit the prifoners, from the impoffibility of the crimes exifting. This found philofophical argument procured a verdict of guilty
from the jury, a fentence of death from the judge,
and perhaps perfuaded the prifoners themfelves that
they really were witches—fo great is the force of
divine eloquence! " Satan's natural knowledge,"
faid the learned council, " makes him perfect in
optics and limning, whereby he may eafily bewitch
the eyes of others to whom he intends that his inftruments fhould not be feen in this manner, as
was formerly hinted, viz. he conftricts the pores of
the witches vehicle which intercepts a part of the

rays

With a few mifcellaneous remarks, which might perhaps have been more properly arranged among the foregoing heads, I will finifh this imperfect fketch of the Brazen-Age.

Society at this period prefents to our obfervation a ftruggle between the un-fubdued ferocity of individuals, and attempts of the chief to make all perfons amenable to thofe regulations which he has

rays reflecting from her body; he condenfes the in-terjacent air with groffer meteors blown into it, or otherwife violently moves it, which drowns ano-ther part of the rays. And laftly, he obftructs the optic nerves with humours ftirred towards them. All which, joined together, may eafily intercept the whole rays reflecting from thofe bodies, fo as to make no impreffion upon the common fenfe. And yet, at the fame time, by a refraction of the rays, gliding along the fitted fides of the volatile couch in which Satan tranfports them, and thereby meeting and coming to the eye, as if there were nothing interjacent, the wall or chair behind the fame bodies may be feen," &c. &c. &c.

has pronounced to be laws—Nor is it
lefs curious to fee with what greater wil-
lingnefs mankind, in this ftate, fubmit to
fuperftitious ceremonies than to reafon.
Truth is not attempted to be difcovered
by an enquiry into facts, but by fuper-
natural means. A wife accufed of adul-
tery, makes no attempt to prove her
innocence from circumftances, but by
walking barefoot over the burning plow-
fhares.* Thievery is to be difcovered
by

* This ancient European cuftom even now pre-
vails in India. In the Afiatic Refearches there are
many inftances of the fiery ordeal being practifed
in and about 1784: and one inftance of a perfon's
grafping a red-hot iron ball, unhurt—An additional
proof of the natural inhabitants of Indoftan being
ftill in the Brazen-Age.

No very accurate obfervation feems neceffary to
know that iron may be hot without changing colour, that a greater degree of heat makes it red,
and by a greater heat ftill, it becomes white—But
the fuperftition of the Kalmucs is more than equivalent for this truth. They hold that in all ordeal
proofs, iron white-hot, burns lefs than iron red-
hot.

by the turning of the fieve and fhears.
Murder by the corpfe frefh bleeding in
the prefence of the murderer. Stars appear upon joyful occafions,* and difaf-
trous events are foretold by comets.✝

Superftition

---

hot. But why fhould I laugh at the Kalmucs?
With us, it is a common notion, that a tea-kettle
full of boiling water may be fafely refted upon the
naked hand. The fact is, if the kettle has been
much ufed, and has a thick cruft at the bottom
of condenfed fmoak, it prevents the heated metal
from coming in contact with the hand; but if the
kettle be new and clean, it is hotter than the water
it contains in proportion to its fuperior denfity.

* " Prince Charles was born at St. James's a
little before one in the afternoon—At his birth, at
that time of day, a ftar appeared vifible—Some faid
it was the planet Venus, others Mercury," &c.

RUSHWORTH.

✝ " A comet appeared (fays the above hiftorian)
to whofe threatenings a learned knight boldly af-
firmed that England (and not Africa only, as fome
out of flattery would have it) was liable; but alfo
that perfon (James the firft) in whofe fortune we

were

Superftition feems to be the leading principle in all their fciences and doctrines,
whether civil, military, or religious.

This darknefs is at times illuminated
by a fingle individual, who fhall by the
ftrength of genius advance beyond his
time and place into a future age of improvement. By fuch perfons does the
world grow better and wifer—but it is
moft commonly the world that fucceeds,
not that which exifts at the time. Roger
Bacon was in genius and knowledge fome
centuries later than the æra in which he
flourifhed. The firft voyage of Columbus
is one of the greateft atchievements in
the hiftory of mankind, but it was an
effort of his own genius, reafon, and in-
trepidity—the age in which he lived dif-
couraged

were no lefs embarked than the paffenger in the
pilots"—Again—" This year Queen Anne died
(wife of James the firft) the common people thinking the blazing ftar rather betokened her death than
the wars in Bohemia and Germany."

couraged his attempt, and was not far,
enough advanced in knowledge to comprehend the reafoning on which it was
founded. Let not therefore thefe inftances, nor the invention of gunpowder
and printing, be brought as examples of
the genius or knowledge of the *age* in
which they were difcovered, but more
truly of the talents of illuftrious perfons
who fhone *fingly* amid the fhades of ignorance.

At this time it is philofophy, which is
the foundation of all our arts and fciences.
As nothing can differ more from fuperftition, if philofophy had not begun very
gently, and advanced by flow degrees, it
would have been ftrangled in the birth.
The idea of accounting for things from
the laws of nature and experiment, was
fo abhorrent to the ignorance and ipfe
dixit of ancient times, that it was affumed
with fear and trembling, and even treated
as wickednefs. Accordingly the firft
philofophers

philofophers were confidered by the world in general, as dangerous innovators, who were, if poffible, to be crufhed, and their doctrines rejected. Notwithftanding we are fo far advanced in refinement, we are ftill a little afraid of philofophical enquiries upon fome fubjects—However, let us be thankful for what we poffefs, nor hope for perfection until that Age arrive of which it is the characteriftic.

Compleatly to inveftigate all the additions to our knowledge fince the commencement of the Silver-Age would require more labour, and greater fources of information, than can reafonably be expected from a fingle author—a flight fketch is all I am capable of or pretend to, which, tho' exceedingly defective, may be of fome ufe in affifting others who are difpofed to compleat thefe enquiries.

Where

Where the fubjects are fo various, the choice is confounded. To take them as they occur, might occafion fome perplexity from an intermixture with each other; and to affect method, might caufe the propriety of my arrangement to be difputed. I will endeavour to avoid the dangers which threaten me, and come off with as little damage as I can.

Bookfellers make out their catalogues and methodize their books under the different heads of divinity, hiftory, law, and phyfic—they fhall be my authority for taking my fubjects in the above order. The arts and fciences may follow, to which fome will be added of a mifcellaneous nature.

The divinity of Queen Elizabeth's times was of that fevere, four caft, which ftill diftinguifhes fome of our prefent fects. If we were to become good, it was lefs from the hope of reward, than

from

from the fear of punifhment. Thefe
rigid doctrines by degrees gave way to
more comfortable tenets, and now many
divines fhocked with the idea of what
feemed to delight our forefathers, I mean
the belief of eternal torments, are ftriving
with great humanity to eftablifh a fyftem more confonant with infinite mercy.
School-divinity is perfectly abolifhed.
All pofitions which cannot be underftood, and if they could be fo, are of no
confequence, have long fince ceafed to
be fubjects of conteft, and almoft to exift.
Our fermons are generally upon the duties of life, or upon fuch fubjects as cannot be controverted; tho' occafionally a
wrong-headed preacher may expofe himfelf in finding hidden and myfterious
meanings in doctrines fufficiently plain,
or which can never be made fo. But
thefe are trifles—the glorious characteriftic of the prefent times, at leaft in England, is, that we are no longer perfecuted for mere opinions, let them be ever

fo

fo abfurd, if they do not affect the good
of fociety. This then is the great advantage of the Silver-Age, and is a broad
foundation on which to build our hopes
of what the Golden-Age may accomplifh.

The hiftorians of the laft fifty years in
England, and the laft feventy in France,
are much fuperior to all others who preceded them. We are fo accuftomed to
treat many ancient authors with refpect,
that we ftill continue our praife, although
they have ceafed to delight us. Yet the
ftyle of Habington has little of the ruft
of antiquity. The Hiftory of the Rebel-
lion by Lord Clarendon is the work of
a man of information and genius, and
Whitlock's Memorials may be trufted for
their honefty. This catalogue might be
much increafed, but there is fuch a hoft
of moderns to match againft them, that
they fink almoft to nothing. The value
of Hume, Robertfon, Henry, and Wat-
fon, will encreafe daily—the mention of
foreign

foreign writers would open too great a field; but I cannot forbear to exprefs my high opinion of Voltaire, who muft not be thought deficient in truth becaufe he abounds in vivacity. Were I difpofed to depreciate one of our famous moderns, it would be an hiftorian whofe reputation is much too great to be hurt by fo feeble an opinion as mine—but in Gibbon the affectation of elegance is always fo apparent, as to prevent us from feeing his learning, impartiality, and other great and good qualities.

The many difcoveries in arts and fciences, the vaft extenfion of commerce, and numberlefs other caufes, have occafioned fuch new combinations in fociety, that every year requires fome regulations unknown to our anceftors. A multitude of laws, without fuch circumftances to produce them, might be juftly confidered as a grievance; but when they are the natural effects of good caufes, they

are

are rather proofs of the progrefs of fociety. There will alfo new crimes arife
which muft be punifhed; and old ones
by being ftill committed, call for additional feverity. Although the penalty
for the breach of fome ftatutes is encreafed, yet, there is a general mildnefs
in thofe of the laft feventy years, and in
the adminiftration of juftice, to preceding
times unknown. The profeffors of the
law in the laft century had a rudenefs of
behaviour and cruelty of difpofition perfectly unfuitable to the prefent times:
of which the trial of Sir Walter Ralegh,
and indeed all other trials for treafon, are
melancholy proofs. No advocate would
now ufe fuch language as Noy did, or
fuch as paffed current for many years
after. Both the laws themfelves, and
the profeffors are tinged with the mild
character which the progrefs of philofophy never fails to eftablifh.

The

The art of phyfic, until lately, feemed
to confift in an affemblage of every horrid fubftance that ignorance and fuperftition could jumble together; which was
formed into bolufes, draughts, and pills,
and forced down the throat of the miferable patient. Every new difpenfatory
finds fomething nugatory, if not hurtful
in thofe before publifhed, and the materia
medica will, by degrees, be reduced to a
few powerful medicines, which will be
adminiftered for the affiftance of nature,
and not to counteract her efforts. Let
us be thankful that in thefe diforders
which occafion fo ardent a defire for frefh
air and water, we are not now ftifled in
a clofe room, nor heated with cordials.
Let us rejoice that phyficians begin to
think themfelves only the fervants to nature. Formerly her dictates were held
in fovereign contempt—perhaps by degrees they may addrefs her like Edmund
in Shakefpeare, " Thou nature art my
goddefs." Already a phyfician has had
the

the courage to write, that a perſon la-
bouring under a diſorder is like a pond of
water ruffled by ſomething caſt into it—
the way to have it ſtill, is not by forcing
the waves to ſubſide; but to do nothing,
and permit gravity to produce its never-
failing effects. It is impoſſible for the
knowledge of medicine to advance, and
that of chirurgery to be ſtationary—they
muſt proceed and improve together. The
modern anatomiſts have partaken of the
improvements of the preſent Age, and
carried their art to a degree of perfection
unknown in times preceding. Reaſon
and true philoſophy, as already remarked,
being the principles upon which our preſent ſyſtem of arts and ſciences is founded,
it cannot be ſuppoſed that modern ſur-
gery ſhould prefer theory to experiment.
If the phyſicians addreſs themſelves to
nature, the ſurgeons obey the dictates of
the ſame all-healing power.

E   The

The science of astronomy must be supposed in a bad state when the Ptolomaic system was considered as the true one. Long after the revival of the system of Copernicus, that of Ptolomy still held its ground, and was believed by so learned a man as Dr. Browne, and not disbelieved by Milton; who, in the conversation between the Angel and Adam, balances between the two theories, not for the reason Addison assigns, but because that of Copernicus was not firmly established.

The true system of the universe was at last confirmed by Sir Isaac Newton, Dr. Halley, with some other contemporary astronomers, and is daily receiving additional strength. Great discoveries have been lately made, and greater still are expected from the vast power of modern telescopes. Could Galileo have imagined what improvements another Age would make in his simple perspective glass, it might have cast a gleam of light

over

over the horrors of his doleful prifon, into which he was thrown for being wifer than the barbarifm of the Age would admit.* Horrox triumphed in feeing firft the tranfit of Venus, but he never imagined that the folar fyftem would have been extended beyond the orb of Saturn —but why do I revert to the time of this ingenious aftronomer? Our prefent philofophers as little fufpected the exiftence of the Georgium Sidus § as their predeceffors.

What

---

* " Virgilius, furnamed Solivagus, a native of Ireland, and Bifhop of Saltzburg, in the 8th century, ventured to affert the heretical doctrine of the Antipodes, and of other planets befides the earth; for which the Pope pronounced his anathema—Galileo then was not the firft philofopher whom the Court of Rome perfecuted."

WATKINSON.

§ Perhaps Dr. Herfchel had juft read the Rape of the Lock, and chofe " to infcribe amid the
ftars

What farther difcoveries are referved for the Golden-Age may be owing to the late-invented inftruments for obfervation; which feem to promife a future intimate acquaintance with the ftarry heavens, in comparifon of which our prefent knowledge may be confidered as ignorance.

The relinquifhing falfe opinions always accompanies the progrefs of real knowledge. Aftronomy has advanced, and Aftrology has retreated—however it held its ground until Butler firft laughed it out

ftars Great George's name"—but, without intending the leaft difrefpect to the King, or to his aftronomer, I may be permitted to remark, that all Europe is diffatisfied with the appellation. In the firft place, Sidus is not the Latin word which anfwers to our idea of a planet.—Again—the reft of the planets have all names of the fame houfe—Mercury, Venus, &c. &c. and the new one might not improperly have taken that of Neptune—if this was rejected, it might have been named from the difcoverer—indeed the propriety of being fo named, is evident from foreign aftronomers always terming it the planet of Herfchel.

out of countenance in his Hudibras,* and the wits of Queen Anne's reign continued the laugh with so much success, that it never more can shew its face in an enlightened country.

Scarce any great undertaking in the last century was begun without consulting the stars. The immediate use which Charles the first made of a thousand pounds sent him at Brentford, was to fee Lilly the astrologer to tell him his fortune—" I advised him," says the Sage, " to march eastward, but he marched westward, and all the world knows the consequence." In Persia this art is still

in

* See the adventure of the Knight with Sidrophel, and numberless other open and covert attacks on astrology dispersed in various parts of the poem. Butler had too much original sense of his own, to join in with popular belief, unless it had truth for its support.

in its full vigour—but Perfia is not the land of knowledge.

As the fciences mutually affift each other, fo ignorance is never demolifhed in one inftance, but it is put to flight in others. With aftrology departed magic and witchcraft; and all the apparitions which terrified our forefathers are va-nifhed for ever!

Our knowledge of metaphyfics before Locke was but little. Whether he ex-haufted the fubject, or whether new light has been thrown upon it by Hartly, Beattie, Prieftley, and others, can never be determined, unlefs the fcience itfelf was capable of fomething like demon-ftration. Perhaps we may confider the old writers as more learned, and the mo-derns more natural. We agree with Locke becaufe we are afraid to differ from him; but we join in opinion with Beattie, becaufe he feems to have brought

down

down his pofitions and arguments to a level with our underftanding.

As natural hiftory depends upon patient enquiries, and the refult of experiments; it muft have been in an imperfect ftate when little attention was paid to fuch fubjects, and few experiments made. It is true that there are fome old books upon this fubject, which may be confidered as hints to future enquiries, and have been ufed as fuch; but the modern additions to natural hiftory are fo very great, arifing from our fuperior opportunities of procuring information, that the works of our predeceffors are of little other ufe, than fhewing the low ftate of the fcience when they were compofed.

The invention of the microfcope opened a new field of enquiry, and from being firft ufed as an inftrument for amufement, became the means of difcoveries unfufpected by times preceding us. Hook in .

E 4   ·   England,

England, and Lewenhoeck in Holland, were indefatigable and very fuccefsful in thefe ftudies; together with other ingenious obfervers, they eftablifhed a tafte for refearches into the minute and hidden parts of nature.

In our Age the moft inconfiderable animal is confidered as an object worth enquiry; and as many perfons have engaged in this line of knowledge, our acquaintance with the different beings that people the globe has moft wonderfully encreafed within a few years.

But tho' by the affiftance of the microfcope, myriads of creatures are found which were not before conceived to exift, it muft not be imagined that microfcopic objects alone engage the attention of the naturalift. The fuperior order of animals, through all their different departments, have been inveftigated with an accuracy and attention unknown to former times.

times. Many new animals have been
difcovered, and fcarce a voyager returns
from geographical refearchcs, who does
not enrich natural hiftory with fome new
addition.

The ftudy of plants is nearly connected
with that of animals. The progrefs and
difcoveries of modern times, in Botany,
would require a much greater length
than this effay, merely to enumerate.
This is of late become a favourite purfuit, and, being one of the various paths
which leads to knowledge, it muft be
confidered to be ufeful as well as agreeable—perhaps, fome are deterred from
proceeding in this track by the found,
and fome by the meaning of the terms.
Admitting the truth of the theory, might
not fuch terms have been ufed as are lefs
pompous, and lefs connected with animal
properties ?

The

The catalogue of new plants has alfo received an immenfe increafe from the late voyagers; and by their bringing the feeds, and in many inftances the plants themfelves to England, our gardens are enriched with objeΦs of ufe, beauty, and curiofity.

It is by no means my intention to take even a curfory review of all the departments of natural hiftory—it may be fufficient to fay, that our progrefs has been great in them all, and chiefly fo within the time fuppofed to be included under this head of the enquiry.

Mineralogy and lithology are fo conneΦed with chemiftry, that our great advances in the knowledge of thefe fubjeΦs we may juftly fuppofe to be in confequence of our application to this noble art; one great fource of the fcience of nature! Lithology is in fome meafure a modern difcovery—I do not mean to fay

that

that our anceftors did not know there were varieties of ftones; but that the inveftigation of the caufes of thefe varieties, and their application to natural hiftory, were referved for the Silver-Age, which has but juft entered on the fubject.

The globular figure of the earth, although formerly fufpected by fome, and believed by a very few, was not generally received until the commencement of the æra which is our prefent fubject. Philofophers, after a long conteft with vulgar prejudices, at laft eftablifhed their point, and the world was acknowledged to be round—every where except in Afia; there they ftill infift upon its being flat, and placed upon the back of an elephant.

Some difcoveries arifing from the vibration of pendulums, which was found to be performed in different times in different latitudes, gave a fufpicion that the

earth

earth was not quite fo round as we imà-
gined. This was proved at laft, and we
have fqueezed the poles a little nearer
together.

Befides afcertaining the real figure of ·
our planet, we have of late been very in-
duftrious to know it better within and
without. Wherever we have an opportunity of penetrating a little way into the
furface of the earth (which fome think is
fearching its bowels) we are attentive to
all we fee and find, and make it fubfervient to the perfecting the theory of its
firft formation, and the changes which
time has produced. We have alfo fent
naturalifts into all the known parts of the
globe, and voyagers to difcover parts
unknown—in fhort, we are doing the
drudgery by which the Golden-Age is
to profit.

Lord Bacon, before the commencement of the Silver-Age, marked the path
for

for his fucceffors in philofophical enquiries. He recommended experiment as
the only true foundation of natural difcoveries, wifely remarking, that we are
not to reafon from preconceived theory,
but what from experiment we find to be
the truth.

This was faid many years before it was
put in practice ; but now, the doctrine is
fo firmly eftablifhed, that we do not attend to any opinion in natural philofophy
unfupported by experiment. It was by
experiment that Boyle fhewed the properties of the atmofphere, and that Newton confirmed all his fublime theories.
Halley took long voyages to perfect, or
deftroy, his ideas of the trade winds,
and variation of the compafs ; for without the fupport of experiment he would
not have ventured to give them to the
public.

When

When Franklyn conceived that lightning and the electrical fpark were the fame; before he would determine the point, he produced the effect of lightning from the difcharge of his electrical battery, and the ufual phænomena of electricity from a filken kite fent up to a cloud. Succeeding enquirers into the nature of this wonderful fluid, have found that the nerves are among its conductors —but this theory requires more experiments for its eftablifhment.

The exiftence of the various Airs has of late much engaged our attention—they (together with electricity) have been applied to medical purpofes, but not with fuch fuccefs as to obtain univerfal approbation.

From this very flight furvey of the fubject, it is evident, that our modern philofophers have far outgone their predeceffors; and that the Silver-Age has made

made difcoveries and a progrefs in the knowledge of nature, of which our an-ceftors, who reafoned only from theory, muft neceffarily have been ignorant.

It would carry this fketch far beyond its propofed limits, to trace the progrefs of the arts from barbarous ages to their prefent ftate; but nothing marks the pro-grefs of refinement fo much, or diftin-guifhes the Iron, Brazen, and Silver Ages fo effectually from each other, as the ftate of the arts. Any production of art is, by the connoiffeur, with the greateft eafe referred to its proper æra—for, if it be impoffible that an artift in the early ftages of fociety fhould anticipate tafte (the great characteriftic of the times which are to fucceed) it is almoft equally im-poffible for a modern to diveft himfelf fo totally of tafte, as to have no tincture of the elegance which we have already acquired.

Thefe

Thefe obfervations principally apply
to the liberal arts, of which we will
flightly remark the moft diftinguifhed
features. The mechanic arts will then
be mentioned, but very imperfectly;
their variety and number rendering fuch
a multifarious fubject impoffible to be
known, unlefs almoft every art had a feparate treatife, and every treatife a feparate author. However, all that is intended will be proved, which is the vaft
fuperiority of the prefent age to the two
ages which have preceded it, and our
progrefs towards perfection.

The arts of painting, fculpture, and
architecture have been carried to a great
degree of excellence in the Silver-Age of
ancient Greece and Rome, of modern
Italy, France and England—but not
equally fo.

It has already been remarked, that Italy
took the lead in refinement—the Age of
Leo

Leo the tenth was in that country an æra
for knowledge and tafte, before even the
terms were underftood in the reft of Europe. By a comparifon of the works of
art produced in a barbarous age with thofe
of enlightened times, it muft appear that
the former are defective in truth and elegance, and many other fubordinate properties. If we reftrict our obfervations
to painting; the works of the Brazen-
Age are deficient in defign, colouring,
drawing, grouping, and every other principle of the art; all which are held, and
practiced as effentials, by the moderns.
From the pictures which have efcaped
the general wreck of time and military
deftruction, we cánnot in juftice think,
that the painters of ancient Greece and
Rome are to be compared with thofe
which flourifhed foon after the revival
of the arts, and thofe which exift at the
prefent time.

The

The fculpture of the Brazen-Age
fhews a very incorrect knowledge of the
human figure, an ignorance of graceful
folds in the drapery—of difpofition of
parts fo as to produce effect for the whole
—and in ornamental foliage, a ftiffnefs
and want of tafte. In our times, every
thing that tends to accuracy and grace is
juftly confidered as the foundation of true
effect, which cannot, to the learned eye,
be produced by other principles.

Sculpture in all its parts was undoubtedly carried to a greater height in Greece
than in ancient or modern Rome, France,
or England. There are fome ftatues and
bufts, and many engraved gems, held to
be fuperior in greatnefs of defign and accuracy of execution to any works of modern times.

The fame bad tafte, which in the preceding age prevailed in painting and
fculpture, was confpicuous in architecture.

ture. The caftles were vaft heaps of ftone, calculated neither for defence nor refidence; the churches were Gothic, a ftyle of building which is certainly bar- barous, notwithftanding fome illuftrious inftances of irregular grandeur;* and the houfes inconvenient and unhealthy, or mere cabins. We, in the Silver-Age, make fortifications which are difficult to be affailed, and eafy to be defended. When we build churches, if we had the fame opportunity and encouragement for exerting our abilities as our anceftors, we fhould produce much better works—of which the principal church at Namur— feveral churches in Paris, St. Paul's in London, and above all, St. Peter's at Rome, are ftriking inftances. Perhaps, architecture was pureft in Greece—its greateft magnificence was in ancient Rome

---

* See fome remarks on Gothic architecture im- mediately following this effay.

Rome—and, in our times, without being deficient in purity or magnificence,
it has the addition of two other principles, comfort and convenience, which
are more attended to in England than in
any other country.

Naval architecture, from this its very
improper term, feems to be connected
with civil architecture, but its ufe and
principles are widely different.

Trees hollowed by fire became veffels
fufficient for the purpofes of navigation in
the firft ages of fociety—in fome countries canoes were formed of leather, and
continue to be fo made upon the Wye—
but if in this inftance we adhere to the
cuftom of our forefathers, we have left
them far behind in the prefent ftructure
of our fhips, which is upon the moft perfect principles of mathematics and me-
chanics, as far as they are yet practiced.

Different

Different nations are conſtantly endeavouring to rival each other in ſhip-building—to conſtruct veſſels of greater force, more tonnage, and ſwifter ſailers. By this conſtant emulation, ſhips have been built uniting theſe properties, which former ages muſt have deemed impoſſible to have accompliſhed. The fleets of the Saxon kings were but row-boats—the great ſhip of Harry the eighth (and ſo named) far exceeded all others hitherto built, and was eſteemed the wonder of the world; yet it was not equal to one of our fourth rates. A modern frigate of forty-four guns would have been an over-match for the ſtouteſt veſſel of Queen Elizabeth's fleet, as a ſeventy-four upon the preſent eſtabliſhment is of ſuperior force to a firſt-rate of the laſt century.

By the natural progreſs towards perfection, ſhip-building would keep pace with the other arts, and we find that it did ſo from hiſtoric facts. Long after

the

the beginning of this century the different rates of men of war proceeded by
round numbers—it was a ship of 20, 30,
40, 50 guns, &c. The French navy
being commonly worsted in their engagements with ours, the force of their
ships was increased—Thus, a 70 gun
ship became a 74 with greater tonnage,
more men, and heavier cannon, and so
of the other rates. This advance of
strength was instantly imitated by the
other maritime powers, so that all having increased, things remained in the
same relative situation as before.* This
must always be the case, so that we contend for superiority in points which must
soon be equal. It is the opinion of the
English, that the French ships sail better
than their own. If this were so, it seems
difficult to account for the French ships
not getting away from ours when it is
- their

* Since writing the above, the Spaniards have
built ships of 130 guns, and the French of 120.—
The English first-rates, as yet, remain as before.

their purpofe to efcape—this fo feldom happens, that we muft fuppofe the opinion is more liberal than juft. As far as I have had an opportunity of obferving, the ornamental carvings at the head and ftern are defigned and executed with much more tafte by the French artifts than by our own.

Engraving is practifed in every country of Europe that has advanced into the Silver-Age, but at this time it is thought to be beft underftood in England. It was in our country that mezzo-tinto was invented, and our artifts in this branch are confeffedly the firft in Europe. It was in England that etching and engraving were firft united, and where the point was firft ufed. Etching, engraving, fcraping, and pointing feem to include every poffible method of producing effect for the taking off impreffions—but let us not fet bounds to human invention—it is the purpofe of this imperfect effay to

F 4   fhew

shew that in all studies, arts, and sciences, we have better times and greater improvements still to expect.

The sinking of dies for coins was in a deplorable state in every part of Europe, except Italy, until within the last 150 years. The savages of New Zealand could produce nothing worse than the pieces of our early Henrys and Edwards. They were improved by degrees, but the principle on which they were formed was quite false, until Simon, in his works for the Protector, gave a specimen how coins should be designed and executed, by taking the Greek for his model, as the Romans had done before him. The moderns have attained to so great a perfection in this art, that they are not unequal to their Roman and Greek predecessors in design, and superior in execution; which may arise from the great advantage of our machinery for coining, over the punch and hammer.

Man

Man, in the earlieſt ſtages of ſociety, ſeems ſenſible to the pleaſure of muſical meaſures before the exiſtence of muſical ſounds. There are many ſavage nations who have no idea of tune, but beat a rhythmus with great preciſion on pieces of wood, with which they mark their ſteps in dancing*—this is the Iron-Age of muſic. The next advance is muſical ſounds joined to the meaſure, which by degrees produces melody, and together with the firſt imperfect attempts towards harmony, or putting parts together, mark

the

* " The negroes (ſpeaking of thoſe at Surinam) in their muſic never uſe triple-time, but their meaſure is not unlike that of a baker's bunt, ſounding tuckety-tuck, tuckety-tuck, perpetually—to this noiſe they dance with uncommon pleaſure."

STEDMAN.

Are we to ſuppoſe from this paſſage that equal meaſure is more natural than unequal? However this may be, it is certain that the common people underſtand ſhort tunes beſt—in a cathedral they like the chant better than the ſervice, and next to that, the reſponſes to the commandments.

the Brazen-Age of mufic. The grace-
fully uniting harmony with melody (in-
cluding meafure, of courfe) is that ftate
of the art to which it is arrived in the
prefent times, the fuperiority of which
over the precedent, is my fubject; not a
differtation on the art.

Modern mufic muft be confidered under the heads of compofition and performance.* I will firft make a few obfervations on the prefent ftate of performance, becaufe it has had a confiderable
influence on our compofitions.

About the beginning of this century
the real art of performance was firft ftudied. Corelli may be reckoned the firft
improver of the violin, and confequently
of the viola and violoncello. It was

many

* I purpofely omit the philofophy of found, and
the mathematical proportion of intervals, as having in fact nothing to do with compofition or performance.

many years later that the hautbois, baf-
foon, French-horn, and trumpet were
ftudied, and later ftill that the different
fort of inftruments was attended to—for
this laft improvement (and many others)
we are indebted to the German muficians.
Handel was the earlieft performer in the
true ftyle of the harpfichord and organ,
which has fince been brought to fo great
a pitch of perfection. The invention of
the Piano-forte is very modern—this inftrument has, not improperly, fuperceded
the harpfichord. The progreffive ftate
of the human powers has produced an
excellence in ftyle, and facility in performance, of which former times could have
no conception.

The cultivation of the vocal powers
has been equally fuccefsful, and although
in fearch of novelty we may fometimes
feize abfurdity, yet the art of finging has
been equally improved with that of inftrumental performance.

Excellent

Excellent performance naturally produces mufic which is to keep pace with
it—for no artift can fhew his fuperiority
over his predeceffors, were his powers to
. be limited by the old mufic; and though
the defire of improvement may lead us
beyond the mark, yet by degrees, we are
brought back again within the bounds of
good fenfe; and, upon the whole, advance nearer to perfection.

In the Silver-Age then, melody has
been united with harmony, and both
have been adorned by grace, tafte, and
expreffion.

If our practice and experience were to
preclude a poffibility of improvement,
the very high antiquity of agriculture
might be fuppofed long fince to have
made it perfect—but, to the great credit
of the prefent Age, the fcience of cultivation is confidered as yet in its infancy,
and that more remains to be difcovered
than

than is yet known. Chemiftry is employed to afcertain the firft principles of
manures, and the philofopher communicates the refult of his ftudies to the
farmer, who adopts or rejects it according
to circumftances, of which the practical
hufbandman is the beft judge—that is,
after making due allowance for old prejudices, which too frequently and fuccefsfully oppofe all improvement. Truth
cannot be expected to advance fmoothly;
let us be thankful that it advances at all.
The general progrefs of fcience is confpicuous in agriculture, which has already brought it far beyond its former
boundaries; and we may reafonably expect, from the attention of the legiflature, to have this progrefs accelerated.

Gardening is a branch of agriculture—
the difcoveries of the latter are for its
advantage; but there are other circumftances which are peculiar to gardening
only. The production of early fruits and
flowers

flowers, in their prefent perfection, is an attainment of the Silver-Age. The vaft addition made to the old catalogue of plants by modern difcoveries and feminal varieties, has given us a new vegetable world, unknown to our forefathers—as the exertion of the fame induftry and ability may caufe the prefent times to be claffed with thofe of ignorance.

Landfcape-gardening is an Englifh art, notwithftanding fome attempts to derive it from China; and it is a modern art, in fpite of the prior exiftence of the garden of Alcinous, and the much older and finer one of Eden. There is more genius and practice required for its proper application than may at firft be imagined. The being in poffeffion of ground gives the owner power, but not ability to lay it out; and it is the exertion of this power that has covered fo much ground with deformity, and brought difgrace upon an art calculated to produce plea-

fure

fure by the creation of beauty. To enter upon its principles makes no part of my defign.

The bare mention of the numerous modern inventions and improvements in the mechanic arts, would take more time and fpace than I can devote to my whole treatife—I mean not to infinuate, that if I had both in profufion, I am capable of treating the fubject. Nor is this any difgrace, as it certainly is much beyond the opportunities of information that can be attained by any one perfon. However, enough may be faid to eftablifh my pofition—that the prefent age is ftill in a rapid ftate of improvement, although already in poffeffion of difcoveries of which paft times could not entertain the moft diftant idea. The application of machinery inftead of the hand, has given an exactnefs and expedition to the mechanic arts, and been the means of fpreading modern manufactures over the world, and

and giving comforts and conveniencies to countries, which elfe, might ever have wanted them. The working of metals by the vaft powers obtained from a falling current of water, or that ftupendous machine the fteam-engine, could not, before the modern difcoveries, have been even fuppofed to exift. That barbarous ages were ignorant of the water-wheel, I mean not to affert; but to the prefent times muft be attributed a thoufand new and ingenious applications of it as a firft power. The fteam-engine, however, is in every refpect new, and in its invention as well as application belongs to the Silver-Age. The various ways by which thefe two powers are applied, and the perfect productions of the joint effects of genius to invent, and ability to execute, in fo many thoufand articles of ufe and elegance, are impoffible to be noticed by the flighteft mention, or comprized in a large volume. Iron has been lately applied to a very new purpofe—the con-
ftruction

ftruction of bridges—for which it feems superior to ftone—for, of the latter material I conceive no arch could be executed of 236 feet fpan, and of 33 only in height above the chord. This ftupendous work, erected at the time of writing thefe obfervations, naturally attracted notice, and occafioned a departure from the intention of not remarking particular inftances. With the mention of another modern performance I will finifh thefe imperfect hints, left " another and another fhould fucceed"—The telefcope of Herfchel! which, whether confidered as an inftance of invention or execution, leaves all other works of the fame nature at an immeafurable diftance!

Great are thefe triumphs of art; nor can we fuppofe that fuch illuftrious inftances will be unnoticed, even when the human powers have attained that degree of perfection which we attribute to the Golden-Age.

G   With

With a few obfervations on the general ftate of things I will conclude this fection.

The progrefs towards perfection may be feen in the face of the country, and the appearance of towns—the increafe of cultivated land, and plantations of trees— the connection of places far diftant, by canals and fine roads—the numberlefs fhips, boats, waggons, and other carriages for ufe and luxury—the quick conveyance by the poft—the fuperior ftyle of modern houfes, and their furniture—of modern ftreets and their pavement—the plenty, eafe, comfort, and luxury which every where furround us—the great alteration for the better in a thoufand other circumftances, affuredly marks the improvement of the prefent age, and gives a promife of a greater degree of perfection ftill to be expected.

As the poets formed a Golden-Age, according to their imagination of what is
good

good or defirable; I may, in my turn, imagine what will be the fituation of mankind, when genius, corrected by fcience, and affifted by reafon and virtue, fhall have produced that improvement of fociety to which it naturally afpires—this is the millennium of philofophy.

The idea of reverfing the order of the Four Ages, by this time, muft have received its fupport, or muft be confidered as chimerical.—To fuppofe, with the ancients, that a ftate of virtue and happinefs could fubfift in the early and ignorant ages of fociety, is contrary to all obfervation; but that the world may grow better as it grows wifer, may be inferred from the property of knowledge to purify the heart while it enriches the mind. There are not many inftances of eminence in art or fcience being attained by vicious perfons—the beft philofophers, poets, hiftorians, and the moft eminent profeffors of the liberal arts, are men of integrity

grity and virtue. When great knowledge and good principles are feparated,
it may be confidered as contrary to the
nature of things, and an exception to a
rule founded on experience. It being
then the tendency of a progrefs in knowledge to produce perfection, let us amufe
our imagination with defigning a picture
of fociety in this ftate, which is the real
Golden-Age, even tho' it never arrives—
for ever approaching, but never touching, like the diagonal line between two
parallels.

War makes a neceffary part of the
character of early fociety, and a confti-
tuent part of it when farther advanced.
It has already been obferved, that an age
may for a time, and in fome inftances,
revert to a more barbarous period; and
by a parity of reafoning, may be advanced
into the times which fhall fucceed. Thus
war may be carried on with a ferocity in
the Brazen-Age that only belongs to the

Iron-

Iron-Age, or with a generofity of manners belonging to a later period. Yet each Age has its fixed character from barbarity to humanity; and war, in fome fhape or other, muft exift in every ftage of fociety, but the laft.

Nothing but that rectitude of intention and action which belongs to times of the greateft degree of refinement, can annihilate war. It will by degrees be perceived, that wars do not often produce the end for which they are undertaken; and when they do, the purpofe attained is not equal to the coft and mifchief. Thus, experience, co-operating with the progrefs of reafon, will at laft overcome that appetite for mutual deftruction by which the nature of mankind is difgraced and the world defolated.

The next great bufinefs of mankind is commerce, which, founded on the fupply of mutual wants, will be free and un-

fhackled

ſhackled with any reſtraints, except ſuch as reaſon and convenience dictate for mutual advantage. Nature has diſpenſed different gifts to different regions, and as art has taken directions in ſome countries which are impracticable in others, it will, by degrees, be perceived that it is for the benefit of mankind rather to remove the various productions of nature and art from one country to another, than endeavour to force productions contrary to climate or the genius of the people. By this interchange of good offices, countries become connected not only by intereſt but by mutual eſteem.

All vain unprofitable ſtudies will ceaſe to be purſued. This end is already partly attained. What was eſteemed learning in the Brazen-Age, is conſidered as ignorance in the Silver-Age. School-divinity was once held to be the height of human wiſdom, and it is now thought the depth of folly. Falſe learning, in all its various

forms,

forms, will gradually ceafe to exift, and no ftudies will be confidered as worthy attention, but thofe which contribute to our pleafure, inftruction, or advantage. As nothing is more fimple, and at the fame time more comprehenfive, than the ideas of protection and obedience, probably our prefent perplexed, myfterious fyftems of divinity, will be reduced to a very fmall compafs, and, by degrees, meet with the fame fate that fchool-divinity has already experienced. Moral philofophy will alfo be much compreffed, and our golden fucceffors will be aftonifhed at the number and bulk of the volumes which have been written on a fubject, which, for every practical purpofe, is fo foon exhaufted ; a few plain maxims, whofe truth is univerfally acknowledged, being fufficient to guide us through the paths of life with eafe and fecurity.

If we trace the art of phyfic from the Iron-Age to the prefent, we fhall fee

· with

with pleafure how the progrefs of reafon
and truth have put prejudice and falfity
to flight—

> " As fteals the morn upon the night
> And melts the fhades away !"

Perhaps, in the Golden-Age, the care to
prevent difeafes may, in great meafure,
fuperfede the ufe of a phyfician ; for as
Iago well obferves, " it is in *ourfelves*
that we are thus, or thus." Difeafes are
created by mifconduct and intemperance,
but in the days of perfection, (and not
'till then) there will be no mifconduct
nor intemperance. If accidents require
affiftance, and art is found neceffary, it
will be confidered not as a director of
nature, but an humble affiftant only—this
is almoft the cafe at prefent, as was obferved in the Silver-Age.

" To chaftife, fo as to prevent crimes
by the influence of example, and to reftore the culprit to fociety by reftoring
him

him to virtue; thefe are the principles which ought to direct the legiflature in its eftablifhment of penal laws"—fays M. Jallet. At prefent, the legiflature feeks no more than to prevent crimes in general, by the punifhment of individuals, but we may fuppofe that the progrefs of virtue will at laft make penal laws unneceffary; for man fins only when reafon ceafes to govern, and we are fuppofing a ftate when it reigns unfettered by cuftom, and unoppofed by folly or vice.

As fcience is an accumulation of ac-quirements by a long fucceffion of indi-viduals, given to the world, and preferved throughout all ages by the art of writing, and more perfectly by that of printing; one man poffeffing former difcoveries, begins where his predeceffors ceafed, and after extending the line of knowledge, leaves it to be farther extended by his fucceffors. If fcience were not in its na-ture infinite, we muft, according to our

plan,

plan, fuppofe it arrived at perfection in the Golden-Age—but, it is no detraction from human capacity to fuppofe it incapable of infinite exertion, or of exhaufting an infinite fubject—in the Golden-Age, the progrefs to perfection will not be checked, but continued to the laft exiftence of fociety.

Studies, which have the different departments of nature for their purfuit, are inexhauftible—every animal, vegetable, mineral, ftone, earth, all natural productions furnifh a field for interefting enquiry; the more we examine, the greater are our difcoveries.

An idea of the formation of the world, and its fubfequent variations, is in fome meafure already attained. This fubject has much attracted the attention of modern philofophers, but longer and more extended enquiries are neceffary to perfect the theory of the globe. At prefent

it

it feems to be eftablifhed, that the fur-face of the earth was once beneath the ocean, and that it has alfo received many modifications from the action of fire—that both fire and water are continually deftroying and new-forming this furface, and moft probably will continue their action to its laft exiftence. The geographical ftudy of the globe muft wait for a more advanced period than the prefent, before it will be compleated. Not much above three centuries have elapfed, fince any attempts of confequence have been made to attain a knowledge of the planet we inhabit, and we are ftill but very im-perfectly acquainted with it. In the Golden-Age thefe entertaining and inte-refting enquiries will attain the certainty and perfection which are characteriftic of that happy æra.

To judge of future improvements in the microfcope and telefcope, by the paft —the time will arrive, when our prefent

inftruments

inftruments will be confidered as firft efforts, if the production of the Herfchel-
lian telefcope may not be confidered as
an anticipation of the period we are defcribing.

Perhaps, fome other power may be
difcovered as forcible and as manageable
as the evaporation from boiling water—
another gunpowder that may fuperfede
the prefent—and other applications of
the mechanical powers, which may make
our prefent wonders fink into vulgar performances.

In poetry, we fhall difcriminate between fubjects capable of being adorned
by numbers, and thofe which are better
expreffed in profe. By rejecting common phrafeology, we fhall appropriate a
language for poetical purpofes, and at
laft attain to unite the correct with the
fublime.

In

In mufic, we fhall feek to exprefs paffion and meafure, by pleafing melody joined with pure harmony, and reject all attempts to impofe on our feelings when drawn from illegitimate fources.

In painting, it will no longer be found impoffible to combine grandeur of defign with the hue and forms of nature, which will be found more perfect than any the invention of man can fupply.* The province of the painter is rather to arrange than to create. Nature produces men, animals, and inanimate objects, but does not often difpofe of them to the painter's fancy.

Architecture will not be flavifhly held in Doric, Ionic, and Corinthian bonds, but formed on fuch aliquot parts as correct judgement, joined with elegant tafte, fhall find moft proper for ufe and grandeur of effect.

If

* See Sir J. Reynolds's Difcourfes paffim.

If the progrefs of human attainments lead at laft to that Golden-Age which the ancients held to be our primitive ftate; the philofopher will confider this as the happy future ftate of fociety—a ftate of reward to the fpecies, not to the indivi-dual—a ftate of blifs, the natural confe-quence of fcientific and virtuous exer-tions.

Thus we have endeavoured to fhew, that nothing but rudenefs can exift in the firft age, that it becomes fmoother in the fecond, and more polifhed in the third; but that we are not to look for the laft degree of refinement, until human na-ture, having proceeded through all the different ftages of improvement, becomes perfectly inftructed by fcience, and pu-rified by virtue.

ESSAYS.

ESSAYS.

On Gothic Architecture.

So much has been written lately on
Gothic Architecture, that I am tempted
to depart from the concifenefs I have hitherto obferved, and to convert what
was intended as a note (fee page 67)
into an effay on a fubject of which I may
be fuppofed to have fpoken too flightly.

The Saxon Architecture may be clearly
traced from the Roman, from which it
differs no more than the Italian language
from the Latin, fo that it may be confidered only as a barbarous corruption of
the old Orders. But the Architecture
usually

ufually termed Gothic, having its principles totally diftinct from the Roman,
muft be derived from another fource. Its
origin has not been fatisfactorily traced,
but its rules, as far as they have a foundation in art, may be afcertained. This
fubject has been treated of by writers
more converfant with it than myfelf—my
intention is not to go over their ground
farther than a few remarks make neceffary, which may not be found in their
works.

To the circle, or portions of it, and to
the right-angle, may be referred the general forms in the Roman and Saxon
Architecture.

From acute arches, or acute angles,
may be derived the general forms of Gothic Architecture—but caprice and whim
are as prevalent as principle.

Warburton

Warburton (in a note upon Pope) conceives that the firſt idea of Gothic Architecture aroſe from obſerving the ef- fect of branches croſſing each other in an alley of trees.*   The reſemblance is un- doubtedly very great, and had before been obſerved by Stukely;‡ if admitted, it only gives a principle for the pillars and roof, and of the inſide only.

A late writer derives this order from the pyramid, which is the moſt general principle,

---

* A Theatre at Paris is conſtructed to repreſent a bower of trees: the interlacing of the branches form the cieling.   As it is uſed for ſummer amuſe- ments the thought is judicious, and the effect pleaſing.

‡ " Gothic Architecture (as it is called) for a gallery, library, or the like, is the beſt manner of building, becauſe the idea of it is taken from a walk of trees, whoſe branching heads are curiouſly imitated by the roof."

STUKELY'S ITINERARY.

H

principle, and applies equally to the outfide, which Warburton's does not.

To both thefe principles it feems neceffary to add (as above-mentioned) the
caprice of the builder; fometimes dictated
by good-fenfe, more frequently by the
barbarifms of the times, but never by
real tafte, becaufe in the ftate of fociety
in which thefe edifices were erected,
Tafte did not exift.*

In thofe buildings erected by the
Greeks and Romans, a general fixed
principle may be eafily traced, and from
which they feldom deviated, unlefs in
the fubordinate parts. The Gothic architects were quite at liberty to do with
their pyramidical principle what feemed
good in their eyes—their arches and pinnacles were more or lefs acute—every
poffible angle, if lefs than a right-angle,

has

---

* See Letter 23—in the Thirty Letters.

has been ufed—every proportion of length to breadth, fo that there are fcarcely any two churches that bear more than a general refemblance to each other—nor would there be even this, but from a conceived obligation to preferve the form of a crofs; to have the altar at the eaft-end, and other fixed religious points which neceffarily produced fome coincidences.

The Gothic architects feem perfectly ignorant of the effect of aliquot parts, and the neceffity of fatisfying the eye by having the maffy parts below, and the flighter ones above. The weft-front of Salifbury Cathedral is a collection of minutiæ, perfectly without principle, in which the architect gave full fcope to his caprice. The effect of grouping fome parts together, and of giving repofe to the eye by the abfence of all ornaments, was unpractifed, perhaps unknown to thefe architects, although an illuftrious

H 2 . exception

exception is in the fpire of the above-
mentioned church, which is kept quite
plain, except where it feems to be bound
round with net-work.

They frequently affected a variety
where the form ought to be repeated.
The church at Laufanne has different
pillars and different ornaments for every
arch, which may alfo be feen in fome
pannels in a very old and curious houfe
oppofite Little-Style, Exeter. The windows of the cathedral in that city not
only vary in the fubordinate, but in the
principal parts; nay, they vary in the
general form and dimenfions. The old
bridge at Exeter, and old London bridge,
had no two arches the fame, this is alfo
the cafe of fo many others, that perhaps
the variation was occafioned from repara-
tions made at different times—admitting
it, yet nothing but caprice or extreme
inattention, prevented the new arches
from being like the old ones. There is
every

every appearance that the Gothic architects were not confined to rule, although
they worked *generally* upon the pyramidical principle—and yet they occafionally
departed from it, as in the inftance of
fquare battlements, which in fuch buildings have always an ill effect. If battlements are neceffary, they are eafily
made pointed, but they are beft avoided.
Radcliffe church at Briftol, and the Abbey
at Bath, have better copings than battlements.

One of the moft prevalent faults in
Gothic buildings is the want of truth in
pofitions—thus, you look through the
vifta of an ayle, and you find the terminating window not in the middle, for
which no poffible reafon can be affigned.
This is a more common fault than is ap-
prehended, and even in buildings noticed
for their beauty. As I recollect, there
are fome inftances of this in Tinterne
Abbey—in Exeter Cathedral there are

many;

many; the eaft windows of the two ayles are not in the middle, nor is the window of the chapel at the north-weft end, which is ufed as the fpiritual court: the two largeft pinnacles of the weft front, tho' in correfponding pofitions, are of very different dimenfions—many inftan-ces of fuch inattention might be found in other churches of this period.

It is a common idea that modern ar-chitects cannot execute a Gothic building —the fact is, that they have feldom fuc-ceeded; but it furely is in their power to make a finer Gothic building than any exifting, by working upon the following principles.—If the form of a crofs be ftill obferved (which has its advantages) let it be fingle—the eaft-end terminating in a niche like the cathedral at Amiens, Canterbury, and many others*—the north and

* Sir C. Wren, fully aware of the effect of the recefs, has with great judgement given it to St. Paul's.

and fouth ends of the tranfept fhould be enlightened with circular windows, like thofe of the Abbey of St. Dennis, and of Weftminfter. The weft end fhould invariably have a large window nearly filling the whole fpace.*

The proportions fhould be aliquot from the general plan to the fubordinate parts, and all upon the principle of fome certain acute angle, and fome certain acute arch, which fhould be adhered to after being firft determined.

The

* Nothing atones for the want of a confiderable window at each end of a large church, except it be terminated with a niche. The effect of the view from the eaft, of the Cathedral at Amiens, is fpoiled by the organ hiding the weft-window. Radcliffé Church and the Chapel at Winfor are fpoiled by the ftopping of windows, the latter indeed is not an inftance exactly to the prefent purpofe, but no pictures fhould be admitted within a Gothic building · if they muft deprive it of light.

H 4

The columns and spaces should be over each other—the more massy, below; and the lighter, above.* .

The application of these principles, with others naturally arising from the good taste of the present age, would produce a Gothic building much superior to any that ever existed.

I have already observed, that modern Gothic churches are generally bad—but this does not arise from the difficulty of inventing or executing Gothic Architecture, but from not taking at first a certain angle and proportion; and mixing principles, which, in their nature, are incompatible. Windows with acute arches will not make a building Gothic, if the other parts are not so—a chapel at Bath has such windows to a flat roof—and the new church of St. Paul, at Bristol, has such

* The reverse is seen in the west front of Salisbury Cathedral.

fuch a mixture of incoherent, capricious forms, as renders it the moft abfurd piece of architecture which ancient or modern times ever produced.

Thefe, and many other inftances of a falfe ftyle, only fhew the want of fkill in the builders, in mixing forms which cannot accord; but by no means prove the impoffibility of fuccefs, if a church were defigned upon the principle of the acute arch and angle, and had its other additions from the good tafte of a modern artift, inftead of the barbarous caprice of antiquity.

Although I am clearly of opinion that a Gothic church might at this time be built greatly fuperior to any of old times, yet I doubt, whether the affociation of ideas, upon which fo much depends, would not be wanting to give it the due effect. Our reverence for antiquity, and our reverence for religion,

in

in fome meafure go together. There is a folemnity attached to an old church, becaufe it is old, which we do not feel in a new church, becaufe it is new. How often has it been remarked of St. Paul's, that although a large and fine building, yet it does not produce the religious effect of a Gothic cathedral—which is undoubtedly true, partly for the above reafon, and partly by our being more ufed to fee the Grecian orders applied to buildings for common purpofes. The language of the prayers is not that of common difcourfe, nor is it the ftyle of authors at this period—it does not fuit with any place fo well as a Gothic church, which our imagination makes to be older than one built after the Grecian orders, becaufe, in our country, they were firft ufed after the Gothic Architecture had been long practifed.

The

The middle way not always beſt.

THE ſafety of taking the middle way
is evident, when we are aſſailed by diſ-
putants, each violent in his cauſe—it is
the moſt, ſecure path while we journey
through life, where the difficulty lies in
ſteering between extremes that are equally
hurtful—and this maxim may be generally applied to morals, philoſophy, and
even to religion itſelf: in all which,
violence and coolneſs are equally to be
avoided. But in the imitative arts, as
they are called, the reverſe of this maxim
is our rule and guide, as appears by an
examination of its effect in painting,
muſic, and poetry.

When we would ſtrike the imagination, which is the end of all the arts, it
muſt

muft be by fomething that operates inftantly, and with precifion—this effect
cannot be produced by mediocrity.

In a picture, the fubject muft be told
with fome degree of violence to arreft the
attention. If it be hiftorical, the figures
muft be eagerly engaged, or they will not
feem to be engaged at all. Strong men
muft be *very* ftrong—beautiful women,
fupremely fo. In landfcape, it is not
fuch an affemblage of objects as we *do*
fee, but fuch as we *wifh* to fee—every
thing muft have a brilliancy and agitation
beyond nature, if we are to think it a
reprefentation of nature.

It is this principle which has eftablifhed
fiery inftead of warm colouring—that
makes the heightening touches of trees
red or yellow inftead of light green—that
makes grey hills, blue—that makes a
front and fide light in the fame picture,
and other extravagancies. As our endeavour

deavour to give a juft reprefentation of nature generally fails of effect, we try to impofe on the imagination, by fubftituting an exaggerated refemblance.

Not only in the fubject, drawing, and colouring of a picture we confider the middle path as dangerous, but there muft alfo be a boldnefs in the touch of the pencil, or all our other elevations above mediocrity will be of no avail. The very effence of Drawings depends upon effects fuddenly produced by broad and full touches.

In mufic, quick and flow movements are diftinctly marked, but what is between both feems uncharacteriftic, and though it often has the power to pleafe, it feldom poffeffes fufficient force to affect us. This remark may be extended to the effect of the piano and forte, and even to the manner of performance.

Poetry,

Poetry, in its very nature, poffeffes an energy fuperior to profe—in thought and language it muft fcorn the fafety of the middle path, and find one more elevated, or perifh in the attempt! If it be dramatic (as I have elfewhere remarked*) the characters muft have a degree of extravagance in language and fentiment much beyond common nature. The dreffes of the actors, and their painted faces, are equally neceffary, for without all thefe exaggerations upon the fobriety of nature, we fhould be too feebly touched to be affected.

In epic poetry the characters muft be like the figures in hiftorical painting: the men fhould be either young and ftrong, or old and feeble. The middle-aged man, if abfolutely neceffary for the ftory, muft of courfe be introduced; but at the time of life when youth is loft,

and

* In the Thirty Letters.

and old-age not attained, the character is unpicturefque and unaffecting. It is fo in common portraits : none have a worfe effect than thofe of middle age.

Perhaps it may be urged againft the truth of the maxim I would eftablifh; that there are in mufic, many movements in moderate time; that there are many landfcapes of fimple nature, and many characters in dramatic, and other poetry, which are excellent, although of that middle clafs which I feem to reprobate.

I can only anfwer, that there is nothing beyond the power of genius; and it is never fo evident, as in producing effect where circumftances are unfavourable.

Perhaps it is the confcioufnefs of this difficulty being vanquifhed, that adds to the pleafure we receive from fuch inftances, and raifes our feelings fo far above mediocrity, that the fenfation is as

much

much elevated as if produced by violence. For one mufician who can make a fimple tune like Carey, there are five hundred who can compofe a noify fymphony like Stamitz. There is no fubject fo eafy for a landfcape-painter as a warm evening—it requires but little fkill to *imitate* Claude, it is the firft effort of the fmatterer in landfcape-painting; but no one ventures upon Ruyfdale's green banks, roads, and puddles of water. There will be a thoufand fuccefsful imitators of Raffaele before another Hogarth will arife. Our prefent hiftorical painters are much nearer their prototype, than any of the burlefque caricature defigners are to their great original. Pitt, in his Tranflation of the Æneid, is a very fuccefsful imitator of Pope—but who dares venture to tell a tale like Prior?

The

The Villa.

CALLING upon a citizen of my acquaintance on a Saturday, I found him and his family juft fetting off for his villa in the country. Having nothing particular to hinder me, I accepted a hearty invitation to make one of the party; and as the ladies condefcended to fubmit to a worfe accommodation than ufual, I fqueezed into the well-filled carriage, which very foberly brought us to the place of our deftination.

A citizen's box by the road fide is fo perfectly known, and has been fo often painted in its dufty colours, that I have no new touches to add—It was one of the thoufands that are in the vicinity of London, with nothing to diftinguifh it from its neighbours.

I

Iɲ

In the evening, as we were taking repeated turns on the fmall fpace of the
garden which permitted it, I believe my
friend perceived an involuntary fmile of
contempt playing about my face, which
he confidered as a reproach on his tafte—
to which he made this reply.

" A Londoner's country-houfe has
been the fubject of much ridicule, and
given occafion to fome excellent papers
in periodical publications, from the Spectator, down to our own times. I have
laughed heartily at the wit and humour
it has produced—but we ftill are in the
fame ftate—and ought to be fo."

I acknowledged that my fmile was occafioned by recollecting thofe humorous
defcriptions to which he alluded; that
admitting the propriety of having a villa;
yet, I faw no reafon why it muft always
poffefs fome points for ridicule—

" Every

" Every reafon, fays he, why it fhould not, if thofe points were ridiculous to the poffeffor; but if fources of enjoyment to *him*, he may excufe their being laughed at by *others*—permit me to offer fomething in defence of thefe our little boxes.

" Should you difpute the propriety of our going into the country at all—I reply, that we return the keener to our bufinefs for having had a little relaxation from it—that change of air and exercife contributes to our health. The hope of future enjoyment gives us prefent fpirits. If you knew the pleafure with which we look forward to Saturday, that is to carry us to the little garden, where we furvey the accumulated vegetation of the days we have been abfent, you would think it a fenfation not to be defpifed.

" From what I have obferved, no perfons *really* enjoy the country but the London citizens. Thofe who poffefs

magnificent

magnificent villas feem infenfible to the beauties in their poffeffion. It is the appetite which gives pleafure to the feaft. If we have this inclination, and it is gratified, there is nothing farther to afk. Touchftone is properly matched with Audrey: the fineft lady in the land could only give him pleafure, and that he receives from his Dowdy.

" But, in my opinion, there is more ftill to be faid for us—Are you fure that a box by the fide of a dufty road, is lefs calculated for enjoyment, than a palace fituated in a vaft park?—My neighbour who poffeffes fuch a palace, like you, wonders at my bad tafte, which he continually abufes, for fear I fhould fufpect that he receives pleafure, when fitting in my window, which he does for hours together (notwithftanding the duft) inwardly envying my happinefs that I can fee the world in motion.

" I

" I have obferved, that the poffeffors
of great houfes have a marvellous affec-
tion to a little parlour !—Is it that the
mind fills a fmall fpace without effort,
and finds the whole within the fcope of
enjoyment; while in a large one, it feems
to be making vain attempts to approach
what is out of its reach? We fancy a little
parlour to come nearer, and be, as it
were, part of ourfelves; while a great
room feems made for more than one, and
to belong not only to us, but to others.
Whether this reafoning be juft or not, it
is certain that you feldom are fhewn a
great houfe, but you are informed that
fome fmall room you were paffing unnoticed, is the place where the owner re-
fides—the grand fuite of apartments is
for ftrangers.

" You know that from our fhops we
fee fucceffive crowds for ever paffing.
Were we to retire to abfolute folitude,
the change would be too great to be re-

lifhed.

lifhed. In fhort, we find by experience, that a fmall houfe and garden, from whence fomething may be feen that excites amufement and attention, is more for our purpofe, than an extent of ground, which offers nothing but the fame objects for ever repeated—it may be well calculated for magnificence; but it fhould be remembered, that our purfuit is relaxation from bufinefs, and fuch relaxation as is attended with fomething we can really underftand and enjoy."

On

On Wit.

HAVING mentioned in my ſhort Eſſay on Taſte * that wit was never ſatisfactorily defined; perhaps it may lead us to ſuſpect a want of preciſion in the idea: which is more natural, than to ſuppoſe ſuch perſons as Locke, Dryden, and Pope, ſhould not have ſagacity enough to define what is ſo well underſtood by the greateſt part of the world.

Locke's Reflection on Wit (as I find it in the Spectator) is, " Men who have " a great deal of wit and prompt memo- " ries, have not always the cleareſt judg- " ment, or deepeſt reaſon. For wit ly- " ing moſt in the aſſemblage of ideas, " and putting theſe together with quick-

I 4   " neſs

* In the Thirty Letters.

" nefs and variety, wherein can be found
" any refemblance or congruity, thereby
" to make up pleafant pictures and agree-
" able vifions in the fancy; judgment,
" on the contrary, lies quite on the other
" fide, in feparating carefully one from
" other ideas, wherein can be found the
" leaft difference, thereby to avoid being
" mifled by fimilitude, and by affinity to
" take one thing for another. This is a
" way of proceeding quite contrary to
" metaphor and allufion; wherein, for
" the moft part, lies that entertainment
" and pleafantry of wit which ftrikes fo
" lively on the fancy, and is therefore fo
" acceptable to all people." Sterne, in
his obfervations on this paffage, has, *in
his manner*, demonftrated, that wit and
judgment, inftead of being feparated, go
together—which is fo far true, that wit
is frequently connected with judgment;
but judgment will not often own wit as
a relation.

Dryden's

Dryden's Idea of Wit (taken alfo from the Spectator) is " a propriety of words and thoughts adapted to the fubject"—on which it is properly remarked, that " if this be a true definition of wit, Euclid was the greateft wit that ever fet pen to paper. Addifon does not give a definition of his own, but feems to approve of Locke's idea of the fubject.

Wit, according to Pope, is

——— " Nature to advantage drefs'd,
What oft was thought, but ne'er fo well exprefs'd."

This does not belong peculiarly to wit, but to all fine writing, where the expreffion is newer and better than the fubject.

If it be the property of a definition that it peculiarly fuits the thing defined, neither of the above can be juft—each differs from the other, and may be applied to other fubjects. The definition about

about to be offered, is of wit only, and cannot agree with any thing elfe.

Wit, then, is the dexterous perfor-mance of a legerdemain trick, by which one idea is *prefented* and another *fubfti-tuted*. In the performance of this trick, an oppofition of terms is *frequently*, though not *always* neceffary. The effect pro-duced is an agreeable furprize, arifing from expecting one thing and finding another, or expecting nothing and having fomething. A juggler is a wit in *things*. A wit is a juggler in *ideas*—and a punfter is a juggler in *words*. Should there be fome inftances of wit, which feem not to agree with this definition; like other particular inftances, they muft be confi-dered as exceptions to a general rule, but not of fufficient confequence to deftroy it. I mention this by way of anticipating and obviating an objection that might poffibly be made; but I declare my ignorance of any example of real wit, which, if properly

perly analized, does not come under this definition—for some things pass for wit, which are not so—humour is frequently mistaken for it—both, it is true, are sometimes blended together; but, by attending to the above definition, and a few observations I shall make upon humour, they may easily be separated, and each set in its proper province. Wit is also frequently joined with a pun—they are easily mingled, for, as is above hinted, a pun is itself a species of wit—it exists upon the same principle, but is formed of less valuable materials—as a word is inferior to an idea.

Let us examine such common pieces of wit as occur, and see whether they conform to my definition.

The trick of wit may be performed without the aid of opposition.

" *I* like port wine, says one, *I* like claret, says another, " what wine do *you* like ?"

like?" fpeaking to a third—" That of other people."

But it may be performed better *with* oppofition.

The weather in July proving wet and ungenial; " when," fays one to Quin, " do you remember fuch a fummer as this?—" Laft winter."

Sometimes there is an oppofition of *terms* joined with an oppofition of *ideas*—

A lawyer making his will bequeathed his eftate to fools and madmen—being afked the reafon—" from fuch," faid he, " I had it, and to fuch I give it."

Wit is now and then mixed with a pun—

" How d'ye like the fhort petticoat of the prefent fafhion?" fays a lady to a gentleman—" extremely," he replied, " I care not to what height it is carried."

Wit

Wit is fometimes mixed with humour—

Two perfons difputing upon religion, one of them reproving his adverfary for his obftinacy, offered to wager that he could not repeat the Lord's Prayer—done, fays the other, and immediately begun, " I believe in God," &c. repeating the Creed throughout very correctly. Well, fays the other, I own I have loft, I did not think he could have done it.

In all thefe examples it muft be perceived, that it is the unexpected change which produces the wit; as in the dexterity of hand, it is fomething unlooked for which makes the trick.

I have juft given an inftance of wit joined with a pun, and another of wit connected with humour—the terms being well underftood I did not interrupt my fubject to explain them, but I have a little to fay upon each.

A .

A pun is upon a fmaller fcale, that which wit is upon a greater. As wit confifts in a dexterous change of *ideas*, fo does a pun in a dexterous change of *words* —the principle in both being the fame, punning ought to be confidered as wit.

Manners, Earl of Rutland, telling Sir Thomas More, that " Honores mutant Mores," the other retorted, that it did better in Englifh, Honours change Manners.

A perfon being afked for a toaft, gave the beginning of the third Pfalm—which was found to be—" Lord How."

Punning then confifts in the dexterous change of the meaning of the *fame* word, or of fubftituting *fome others*, which to the ear convey a likenefs of found. " I am come to fee Orpheus," fays a gentleman at the Theatre (in boots)—" yes," fays his friend, " and You-rid-I-fee."

The

The effence of a pun confifts in fome fuch changes as thefe : therefore, if it be admitted that it is the dexterous change which conftitutes wit, punning poffeffes the change and the dexterity.

Humour has no fuch change, but con-fifts either of treating a grave fubject lu-dicroufly, or a light one gravely—if the fubjects admit of being fo treated. The Tale of a Tub is a humourous fatire on the abfurd tenets of religious fects, not on religion itfelf—the former may, with-out offence, be connected with humour, but the laft is in its nature above it.

The moft perfect humour exifts in Shakefpeare,* Swift, and Addifon, and in many writers among the moderns : no inftances of which will be found to be wit, if tried by the above rule. An idea
has

* Shakefpeare abounds in humour, fometimes pure, more frequently mixed with puns—but has not many inftances of real wit.

has prevailed, that humour is only known in England: this cannot be true—Cervantes, Voltaire, and many other foreign writers, afford proofs to the contrary.

There feem to be fome fubordinate fources of humour which are not eafily to be accounted for. Intemperance, no doubt, is an odious vice, and every delicate mind muft be offended at it—but, drunken-characters in a play have frequently a humourous and laughable effect—Sir John Brute, and the Drunken-Man in Lethe, are ftrong inftances.

The Irifh brogue is furely no fubject for ridicule—a man born in Ireland muft of courfe fpeak like his neighbours—but on the ftage it is a never-failing fource of humour—diveft an Irifh character of the brogue and it becomes nothing.

Stammering, by fome means or other, has a connection with humour, efpecially

if

if imitated on the ftage, as we find from Serjeant Bramble, in the Confcious Lovers—but, to return to my fubject.

True wit, fays Voltaire, is univerfal—it is fo, provided all nations are in equal poffeflion of the circumftances which attended its production, and which necef-farily accompany it. There are few pieces of wit, but are, in fome meafure, local. The fprightly fallies in converfa-tion are not only local, but temporary; yet they are as truly wit for the time and place, as the moft general fubject would be for the univerfe, and would be fo acknowledged, if explained and underftood. Many a witty reply owes all its force to fome allufion only known to the company, or perhaps to one fingle perfon—explain that circumftance, and the wit would be univerfally confeffed.

Some expreffions pafs for wit which certainly belong to a different clafs.

K

A

A foldier, finding a horfe-fhoe, ftuck it into his girdle—a bullet hit him on the very part. " Well, fays he, I find a little armour will ferve the turn, if it be but rightly placed." A fenfible reflection, but not wit.

Garrick afked Rich. " how much Covent-Garden houfe would hold?" " I fhould know to a fhilling, replied Rich, if you would play Richard in it." An elegant compliment, and better than wit.

Having, perhaps, thrown fome light on this fubject, I will leave it to the reader's fagacity to improve thefe fhort hints, and compleat what I have haftily fketched—but, before I conclude, permit me to give an inftance of wit combined with humour and pun, and the rather, as it ftands in need of a flight introduction, which will ferve as a proof of local wit becoming univerfal, when rightly underftood.

When

When the Jefuits were difperfed, Voltaire's Chateau afforded an afylum to one of them, an inoffenfive prieft called Adam. " Give me leave," fays Voltaire to his company, " to introduce to you Father Adam—but not *the firft of men*"— it is fhort, but comprehends more than may appear at the firft glance.

After having, I hope, proved that a wit is a jugler ; I do not think it neceffary to prove, that a jugler is a wit, it being a felf-evident propofition, if we admit the principle I have endeavoured to eftablifh, of *both depending on a fubftitution of one thing for another by a dexterous change.*

An

An Indian Tale.

WHEN the hofts of the mighty Timur
fpread from the deferts of Tartary over
the fertile plains of Indoftan, numerous,
and deftroying as locufts; their chief,
glorying in the greatnefs of his ftrength,
furveyed with an averted look the mountains he had paffed, and fmiled at the
barrier he had furmounted. " By forti-
tude and valour, faid he, we fubdue our
enemies; by patience and perfeverance
we overcome even the ftupendous works
of nature, which has elevated mountains
in vain, to ftop the progrefs of him determined to conquer!" While his heart
dilated with pride, the foldiers ravaged
the country through which they, paffed,
committing all the exceffes an unrefifted
army inflicts on the wretched inhabitants.
—" Bring

—" Bring me to your chief," exclaimed
a fage they had dragged from his retreat,
" let me behold this mighty conqueror
before my eyes are clofed in endlefs night;
perchance the words of Zadib may enter
his ears—may reach his heart !"

The air of dignity with which he uttered this, arrefted the fword of the foldiers—" Behold," faid they to Timur,
" a man of years who feeketh thy prefence." " My defire," faid Zadib, " is to
confer with the mighty Scythian—he is
great, but will not turn afide from the
wifdom of experience." " Speak freely,"
replied Timur, " an enemy incapable of
refiftance I treat as a friend—enter with
me this Temple of Viftnoo—inftruction
cannot be heard amid the noife of a paffing army."

" The filence of this facred place,"
begun Zadib, " is favourable to my fubject—O Viftnoo endue thy votary with
confidence

confidence to utter the words of truth before this leader of armies, and prepare his mind to receive thy wifdom ; of which my tongue is but the feeble organ !" "Viftnoo," fays Timur, " is no God of mine, but a benefit is always to be received with gratitude—if I profit from his infpiration, this temple fhall flame with my offerings."

" What could induce the chief," commenced Zadib, " of the wide-extended plains of Tartary, to leave the habitation of his progenitors, and feek in lands remote for what his own fo much better afforded ?—Are the paftures of Indoftan more fertile than thofe of Scythia, is the milk of our mares more plentiful, or the flefh of our horfes fuperior to thofe of the country which gave thee life ? No, thefe things are not fo—the burning fun fcorches our herbage, our cattle yield but little milk, nor afford flefh worthy the hunger of a Tartar. Why then doft

thou

thou inflict the miseries of war on the innocent inhabitants of this country, at the loss of so many enjoyments to thyself?" "To increase my glory!" sternly replied Timur, "the desire of glory is the passion of us who are elevated into the rank of heroes; for *this* we thirst, for *this* we we hunger, and leave to common mortals the flesh and milk of mares!"

"If the desire of glory cannot be gratified but by the destruction of mankind," meekly returned Zadib, "surely it had better be repressed—what good can arise from glory that is to be compared to the mischief by which it is attended?" "Thou talkest like a sage and a philosopher," said Timur more mildly, "and desirest to make man as he should be, which is impossible—my part to act, is that of a prince, who considers man as he is; and who treats mankind, as every individual would treat *him*, had he the same means in his power. It is destiny, and the im-

K 4   provement

provement of opportunity, that makes a tyrant—thofe to whom fate is averfe, muft fubmit and be filent."

"Brahma forbid!" exclaimed Zadib: "None can withftand deftiny; but what virtuous man would feek an opportunity to lord it over his fellow-mortals?" "Be affured," returned Timur, "that virtue is an acquirement. Man, by nature, is felfifh and cruel; all infants are fo—thefe natural paffions are by education oppofed, and by degrees concealed; but never per-fectly fubdued—my defire for glory, then, is affifted by my original paffions of cru-elty and felfifhnefs; which, by being a prince, I can extend to the utmoft."

"If, by being a prince," faid Zadib, "I muft, from neceffity, be cruel and felfifh—may the humble ftate be ever mine!"—"Man alfo poffeffes a defire for fuperiority," continued Timur, "which produces a wifh for fplendor and riches.

By

By nature all are equal, but circumstances have fixed thee in a station where desires must be restrained, and have placed me where they may be indulged—could we change conditions, be assured, thy passions would expand as soon as their restraint was taken off, and thou wouldst be then, as Timur is now."

" Can a worm of the earth be proud ?" humbly replied Zadib,—" What is man but an atom, which can only be considerable by virtue ? When I consider this, I avoid the first approach of pride, and abhor that wicked principle which seeks its gratification by the misery of others." " Call not a conqueror wicked," returned Timur sharply, " he is simply *a man*—he has an opportunity of shewing his nature undisguised, and uses it. The sage is something more, and something less than man. He is more, as he has added to the gifts of nature; he is less, by discarding his natural propensities; but

they

they retire no farther than to be within call"—

"They are difcarded for ever!" uttered Zadib. The fuddennefs of the reply occafioned, for a while, a paufe in this moral and philofophical conference, in which neither party gained on his adverfary—at length Timur, with complacence, broke filence—"Zadib," faid he, "thy good qualities fhall no longer be hidden in obfcurity—thou fhalt be my Vizir—be it my bufinefs to fubdue, and thine to govern."

"Unworthy of the high honour as I am," replied Zadib, his eyes fparkling with pleafure; "yet fhall thy flave endeavour to difcharge the duties of fo great a function." "But doft thou reflect," faid Timur, "that the higher the ftation, the greater is the fcope for vice? Thou art now low, poor, and virtuous; but when thou art the fecond perfon in my empire,

empire, thou wilt be great, rich, and wicked"—" That philofophy I have early acquired," replied Zadib, " fhall fecure me from the firſt approaches of vice—inveſt me with the robe of honour, and be confident of my obedience to thy high commands."

" Zadib," returned Timur, " thou muſt now be convinced, that original pride, and a wiſh for greatneſs, lay lurking within thee, and was never effaced— that thy virtue is an artificial acquirement, which vaniſhes before the original impreſſions of nature—but why ſhould I proceed? Thy heart bears witneſs to the truth of my words, for the bluſh of conſcioufneſs is on thy face—reply not—I will give thee no opportunity to loſe what thou haſt with ſo much difficulty acquired, for the man of nature muſt ſoon appear—thou feeſt him in *me!*—go in peace to thy cell—go, and continue to be virtuous—but leave me to lead on my
victorious

victorious Tartars, until I acquire that glorious appellation, THE CONQUEROR OF THE WORLD!"

Different

Different Ufes of Reading and Converfation.

IN barbarous times, when converfation had no other topic than what immediate occafion or necessary employment produced (which was once the cafe) it is evident, that no knowledge could be obtained but from books.

As civilization advanced, and commerce produced focial intercourfe, converfation grew more enlarged, and knowledge was gained from the mouth as well as from the pen. This undoubtedly was an improvement in every fenfe. In France both fexes firft affembled on an eafy footing, and it was in that country where knowledge from books was firft neglected.

This

This principle fpread with the language and manners, and it foon became fafhionable to call the learning acquired from reading, pedantry. As I confider this to be the prefent ftate of things in our own country, I have a few words to fay in defence of the inftruction obtained from books, and to give fome reafons why it ought, for all fubftantial purpofes, to be preferred to that which arifes from converfation.

The object of converfation is entertainment—the object of reading is inftruction. No doubt, converfation may inftruct, and reading may entertain; but this occafional affumption of each other's characteriftic, only varies the principle, without deftroying it.

When perfons converfe, deep difquifition is out of place—the fubjects fhould be general and light, in which all may be fuppofed capable of joining. Every
thing

thing profeffional is avoided, which, whether from the divine, the lawyer, the
phyfician, the merchant, or foldier, is
equally pedantic as from the fcholar.
All debate is fhunned, left warmth might
become heat. If fire be produced by the
collifion of fentiments, it fhould juft fhine
for a moment, like the harmlefs coruf-
cations of a fummer evening, but not
pierce like lightning.

Converfation, to be agreeable, fhould
be divided equally—no one fhould en-
grofs it, or neglect to furnifh his quota—
but as it requires fome practice, and perhaps, talents, to engage in fmall-talk,
without afcending into an upper region,
or finking into vacuity; thofe who find
a difficulty in fteering this middle courfe,
and think it neceffary to keep up the
fhuttle-cock of converfation; occafionally
hazard an expreffion, which will not
bear ftrict examination, but it may appear fufficiently like truth for the prefent
purpofe,

purpofe, and to be adopted as fuch hereafter. Truth is fometimes overcome by
wit—a lively repartee will at any time
put it to flight. Strength may crufh and
kill, but fmartnefs makes the ftroke to
be felt.

In converfation it is not eafy to avoid
falfities. A ftory is begun, of which the
relator has only a general knowledge—
as he proceeds, he is obliged to fill up
the deficiencies of memory by invention;
the next relator does the fame, and probably, in different places. After a few
of thefe oral editions, truth is entirely
fupplanted by falfehood. If this happen
when there is no intention to deceive,
what muft be the effect when the variation is not accidental ?

To difcover truth is feldom the intention of converfation. Should a difpute
arife, its object is not to eftablifh facts,
but to obtain victory. If the maxims of
our

our great moralift were to be taken from topics he has defended, or contradicted in company, he muft be confidered as the moft abfurd of mortals—this might be fport to him, but it was death to others : the worfhippers of this idol confidering him as a real divinity, and his words as oracles.

Thefe circumftances, and many others not enumerated, very much difqualify converfation from being a fchool of inftruction. If we wifh for real information, we muft undoubtedly feek it from its old fource.

As converfation is furnifhed from the impulfe of the moment; books confift of digefted thoughts, which are felected from many others—thefe are improved, added to, or curtailed, upon mature and frequent deliberation—the author is hurried into nothing, but whatever his ideas are upon the fubject he has chofen,

L   he

he may give them that order and expreffion which will fhew his meaning
cleareft and beft. And furely it cannot
admit of a moment's doubt, whether mature conceptions, put into form, are not
fuperior to expreffions from accident, and
momentary impulfe—not to mention the
multitude of fubjects, which, in company, will not admit of any difcuffion.

We may then venture to affert the
fuperiority of books over converfation,
where inftruction is the object; without
having the leaft intention of depreciating
the pleafures of fociety.

Character

Character of Gainsborough.

IN the early part of my life I became acquainted with Thomas Gainsborough the painter; and as his character was, perhaps, better known to me than to any other person, I will endeavour to divest myself of every partiality, and speak of him as he really was. I am the rather induced to this, by seeing accounts of him and his works given by people who were unacquainted with either, and, consequently, have been mistaken in both.

Gainsborough's profession was painting, and music was his amusement—yet, there were times when music seemed to be his employment, and painting his diversion. As his skill in music has been celebrated, I will, before I speak of him as a painter,

L 2   mention

mention what degree of merit he pro-
feffed as a mufician.

When I firft knew him he lived at
Bath, where Giardini had been exhibiting his *then* unrivalled powers on the
violin. His excellent performance made
Gainfborough enamoured of that inftrument; and conceiving, like the Servant-
maid in the Spectator, that the mufic lay
in the fiddle, he was frantic until he poffeffed the *very* inftrument which had
given him fo much pleafure—but feemed
much furprized that the mufic of it remained behind with Giardini!

He had fcarcely recovered this fhock
(for it was a great one to *him*) when he
heard Abel on the viol-di-gamba. The
violin was hung on the willow—Abel's
viol-di-gamba was purchafed, and the
houfe refounded with melodious thirds
and fifths from " morn to dewy eve !"
Many an Adagio and many a Minuet were
begun

begun, but none compleated—this was wonderful, as it was Abel's *own* inftrument, and therefore *ought* to have produced Abel's own mufic !

Fortunately, my friend's paffion had now a frefh object—Fifcher's hautboy— but I do not recollect that he deprived Fifcher of his inftrument : and though he procured a hautboy, I never heard him make the leaft attempt on it. Probably his ear was too delicate to bear the difagreeable founds which neceffarily attend the firft beginnings on a wind-inftrument. He feemed to content himfelf with what he heard in public, and getting Fifcher to play to him in private—not on the hautboy, but the violin—but this was a profound fecret, for Fifcher knew that his reputation was in danger if he pretended to excel on two inftruments. *

The

* It was at this time that I heard Fifcher play a folo on the violin, and accompany himfelf on the

fame

The next time I faw Gainfborough it was in the character of King David. He had heard a harper at Bath—the performer was foon left harplefs—and now Fifcher, Abel, and Giardini were all forgotten—there was nothing like chords and arpeggios! He really ftuck to the harp long enough to play feveral airs with variations, and, in a little time, would nearly have exhaufted all the pieces ufually performed on an inftrument incapable of modulation, (this was not a pedal-harp) when another vifit from Abel brought him back to the viol-di-gamba.

He now faw the imperfection of fudden founds that inftantly die away—if you wanted a *ftaccato*, it was to be had by a proper management of the bow, and you might alfo have notes as long as you pleafe. The viol-di-gamba is the only inftrument,

fame inftrument—the air of the folo was executed with the bow, and the accompaniment *pizzicato* with the unemployed fingers of his left hand.

inftrument, and Abel the prince of muficians!

This, and occafionally a little flir-
tation with the fiddle, continued fome
years; when, as ill-luck would have it,
he heard Crofdill—but, by fome irregu-
larity of conduct, for which I cannot account, he neither took up, nor bought,
the violoncello. All his paffion for the
Bafs was vented in defcriptions of Crofdill's tone and bowing, which was rap-
turous and enthufiaftic to the laft degree.

More years now paffed away, when
upon feeing a Theorbo in a picture of
Vandyke's; he concluded (perhaps, bé-
caufe it was finely painted) that the The-
rbo muft be a fine inftrument. He recollected to have heard of a German
profeffor, who, though no more, I fhall
forbear to name—afcended *per varios*

gradus to his garret, where he found him at dinner upon a roasted apple, and smoking a pipe—* * * says he, I am come to buy your lute—

" *To pay my lude!*"

Yes—come, name your price, and here is your money.

" *I cannod shell my lude!*"

No, not for a guinea or two, but by G— you must sell it.

" *May lude ish wert much monnay! it ish wert ten guinea.*"

That it is—see, here is the money.

" *Well—if I musht—but you will not take it away yourshelf?*"

Yes, yes—good bye * * *

(After he had gone down he came up again)

* * * I have done but half my errand— What is your lute worth, if I have not your book?

" *Whad poog, Maishter Cainsporough?*"

Why, the book of airs you have composed for the lute.

" *Ah,*

" *Ah, py cot, I can never part wit my
poog !*"

Poh ! you can make another at any
time—this is the book I mean (putting
it in his pocket)

" *Ah, py cot, I cannot*"—

Come, come, here's another ten gui-
neas for your book—fo, once more, good
day t'ye—(defcends again, and again
comes up) But what ufe is your book to
me, if I don't underftand it ?—and your
lute—you may take it again, if you won't
teach me to play on it—Come home
with me, and give me my firft leffon—

" *I will gome to marrow*"

You muft come now.

" *I mufht trefs myfhelf.*"

For what ? You are the beft figure I
have feen to day—

" *Ay mufht be fhave*"—

I honour your beard !

" *Ay mufht bud on my wik*"—

D—n your wig ! your cap and beard
become you ! do you think if Vandyke

was

was to paint you he'd let you be
fhaved?—

In this manner he frittered away his
mufical talents; and though poffeffed of
ear, tafte, and genius, he never had application enough to learn his notes. He
fcorned to take the firft ftep, the fecond
was of courfe out of his reach; and the
fummit became unattainable.

As a painter, his abilities may be con-
fidered in three different departments.
　　Portrait,
　　Landfcape, and
　　Groups of Figures—to which muft be
added his Drawings.
　　To take thefe in the abovementioned
order.

The firft confideration in a portrait,
efpecially to the purchafer, is, that it
be a perfect likenefs of the fitter—in
this refpect, his fkill was unrivalled—
　　　　　　　　　　　　　　the

the next point is, that it is a good picture—here, he has as often failed as succeeded. He failed by affecting a thin washy colouring, and a hatching style of pencilling—but when, from accident or choice, he painted in the manly substantial style of Vandyke, he was very little, if at all, his inferior. It shews a great defect in judgment, to be from choice, wrong, when we know what is right. Perhaps, his best portrait is that known among the painters by the name of the *Blue-boy*—it was in the possession of Mr. Buttall, near Newport-market.

There are three different æras in his landscapes—his first manner was an imitation of Ruysdael, with more various colouring—the second, was an extravagant loosenefs of pencilling; which, though reprehensible, none but a great master can possess—his third manner, was a solid firm style of touch.

At

At this laſt period he poſſeſſed his greateſt powers, and was (what every painter is at ſome time or other) fond of varniſh. This produced the uſual effects—improved the picture for two or three months; then ruined it for ever! With all his excellence in this branch of the art, he was a great manneriſt—but the worſt of his pictures have a value, from the facility of execution—which excellence I ſhall again mention.

His groups of figures are, for the moſt part, very pleaſing, though unnatural—for a town-girl, with her cloaths in rags, is not a ragged country-girl. Notwithſtanding this remark, there are numberleſs inſtances of his groups at the door of a cottage, or by a fire in a wood, &c. that are ſo pleaſing as to diſarm criticiſm. He ſometimes (like Murillo) gave intereſt to a ſingle figure—his Shepherd's boy, Woodman, Girl and pigs, are equal to the beſt pictures on ſuch ſubjects—his Fighting

ing-dogs, Girl warming herfelf, and fome others, fhew his great powers in this ftyle of painting. The very diftinguifhed rank the Girl and pigs held at Mr. Calonne's fale, in company with fome of the beft pictures of the beft mafters, will fully juftify a commendation which might elfe feem extravagant.

If I were to reft his reputation upon one point, it fhould be on his Drawings. No man ever poffeffed methods fo various in producing effect, and all excellent—his wafhy, hatching ftyle, was here in its proper element. The fubject which is fcarce enough for a picture, is fufficient for a drawing, and the hafty loofe handling, which in painting is poor, is rich in a tranfparent wafh of biftre and Indian ink. Perhaps the quickeft effects ever produced, were in fome of his drawings —and this leads me to take up again his facility of execution.

Many

Many of his pictures have no other merit than this facility; and yet, having it, are undoubtedly valuable. His drawings almost rest on this quality alone for their value; but possessing it in an eminent degree (and as no drawing can have any merit where it is wanting) his works, therefore, in this branch of the art, approach nearer to perfection than his paintings.

If the term *facility* explain not itself; instead of a definition, I will illustrate it.

Should a performer of middling execution on the violin, contrive to get through his piece, the most that can be said, is, that he has not failed in his attempt. Should Cramer perform the same music, it would be so much within his powers, that it would be executed with ease. Now, the superiority of pleasure, which arises from the execution of a Cramer, is enjoyed from the facility of a
Gainsborough.

Gainſborough. A poor piece performed by one, or a poor ſubject taken by the other, give more pleaſure by the *manner* in which they are treated, than a good piece of muſic, and a ſublime ſubject in the hands of artiſts that have not the means by which effects are produced, *in ſubjection to them.* To a good painter or muſician this illuſtration was needleſs; and yet, by them *only*, perhaps, it will be felt and underſtood.

By way of addition to this ſketch of Gainſborough, let me mention a few miſcellaneous particulars.

He had no reliſh for hiſtorical painting —he never ſold, but always gave away his drawings; commonly to perſons who were perfectly ignorant of their value.*

He

* He preſented twenty drawings to a lady, who paſted them to the wainſcot of her dreſſing-room. Sometime after ſhe left the houſe: the drawings, of courſe, become the temporary property of every tenant.

He hated the harpfichord and the piano-
forte. He difliked finging, particularly
in parts. He detefted reading; but was
fo like Sterne in his Letters, that, if it
were not for an originality that could be
copied from no one, it might be fuppofed
that he had formed his ftyle upon a clofe
imitation of that author. He had as
much pleafure in looking at a violin as
in hearing it—I have feen him for many
minutes furveying, in filence, the per-
fections of an inftrument, from the juft
proportion of the model, and beauty of
the workmanfhip.

His converfation was fprightly, but
licentious—his favourite fubjects were
mufic and painting, which he treated in
a manner peculiarly his own. The common topics, or any of a fuperior caft, he
thoroughly hated, and always interrupted
by fome ftroke of wit or humour.

The

The indiscriminate admirers of my late friend will consider this sketch of his character as far beneath his merit; but it must be remembered, that my wish was not to make it perfect, but just. The same principle obliges me to add—that as to his common acquaintance he was sprightly and agreeable, so to his intimate friends he was sincere and honest, and that his heart was always alive to every feeling of honour and generosity.

He died with this expression—"We are all going to Heaven, and Vandyke is of the party"—Strongly expressive of a good heart, a quiet conscience, and a love for his profession, which only left him with his life.

M   *Character*

Character of Sir Joshua Reynolds.

IN a short time after the loss of Gainf-borough, the world sustained a greater by the death of Sir Joshua Reynolds. My acquaintance with him and his works enable me to give a sketch of both, which, if short, shall be faithful.

Sir Joshua had the reputation of being a man of genius and knowledge, in his profession and out of it—to deny this would be absurd, but our assent must not be an implicit faith. I will first enquire into his merits as an artist, and then as a man of general science.

He began his profession as a portrait painter, and his works were soon distin-guished by an elegance of design that had

not

not been feen in England fince the time of Kneller. To balance this excellence, his likeneffes were frequently defective, and his colouring cold and weak—but this muft be confidered only as the general character of his performances at that time; for even in his earlieft days, there were inftances of his producing pictures of confiderable merit.

A very few years had elapfed, before it was obferved, that his pictures were changed from their original hue; and the change, in fome, was fo great, as to occafion a belief that the colours were gone off. Perfons, who are ignorant of the mechanical part of painting, reported, that Reynolds knew not how to fix his colours, and that his pictures, in a fhort time, would ceafe to exift. As this matter has never been underftood, I will ftop a moment to explain it.

The

The dead-colouring* of his pictures, at this period, was little elfe than flake, Pruffian blue, and lake. All the laying-in confifted of thefe three tints. When the picture was quite dry, he gave it a warm glaze, which fupplied all that was originally wanting, and produced a harmony in the whole, which was very agreeable and feducing to the eye, when frefh done—but after a while, the drying-oil, (fometimes exchanged for varnifh) with which the pictures were glazed turned dark; and, by degrees, grew more and more obfcure, until the effect was as bad as if they had been covered with a dirty piece of horn. There are great numbers where the face can fcarce be diftinguifhed, and where the drapery is entirely hidden with this brown cruft.

The colours then, are not gone off, but imprifoned—they are obfcured beyond

---

* It is impoffible to write on Art without ufing technical terms.

yond the reach of art to reftore; and all
pictures of this defcription, will continue
to grow worfe and worfe, until the change
of the oil, or varnifh, has attained its
maximum.

This practice (of depending fo much
upon glazing) occafioned the painters to
whifper, that Reynolds did not paint *fair*,
and that he dealt too much in trick.

I dare fay that the fevereft cenfures
came from himfelf; and he, at laft, grew
tired of a practice which he knew muft
obftruct his progrefs to fame, and began,
at laft, to paint *honeftly*.

The firft picture that I recollect, after
this change in his manner, was the portrait of the Lord Primate of Ireland—admirable in every refpect! It was followed by many others truly excellent;
and he continued in this ftyle for many
years.

As

As he poffeffed fome pictures of Rubens, and might fee as many as he pleafed, it was difficult not to be feduced by their fplendor. I once heard him fay, " that a fingle picture of Rubens was enough to illuminate a room!" There is fomething like an emanation of glory from a fine picture of this mafter, which is felt and adored by a kindred genius. In one of the churches at Antwerp is a picture of Rubens, at the High Altar, which feems to be feen by its own light, at the farther end of the church.

This magic of colouring was the favourite purfuit of Sir Jofhua for the laft ten years of his life: but, like other eager purfuers, he was not always in the right track. He may furely be fuppofed wrong, when, to obtain force, he loaded his lights with fo great a quantity of colour, that the different layers and touches
frequently

frequently feparated from the ground, merely by their weight.*

This excefs he wifely abandoned, and long before his death he confidered pictures, not as models, but furfaces.

It was at this period of his practice that he introduced the red fhadows of Rubens; which, though unnatural, are the chief caufe of the fplendor of the pictures of that mafter. Gainfborough once dealt in red fhadows; and as he was fond of referring every thing to nature, or where nature was not to be had, to fomething fubftituted for it,‡ he contrived

* I once heard him *bleffed* by a houfe-maid, who faid (wiping the floor) " that the ftuff which was always falling from that great picture made the room in a perpetual litter! I wifh it would all come down at once!"

‡ He made little laymen for human figures. All the female figures in his Park-fcene he drew from doll of his own creation. He modelled his horfes

M 4   and

trived a lamp with the fides painted with vermillion, which illuminated the fha- dows of his figures, and made them like the fplendid impofitions of Rubens.

After Sir Jofhua had abated fomething of the violence of thefe fhadows, he was in the zenith of his art. It was at this period he produced his Venus and the Death of Cardinal Beaufort, which will make his name equal with the greateft mafters. Of the Venus there is a dupli- cate with fome fmall variation. The co- louring is at leaft equal to Titian, but much fuperior to that painter in elegance of defign. The Cardinal Beaufort has a warm glaze, which is rather too apparent.

He

and cows, and knobs of coal fat for rocks—nay, he carried this fo far, that he never chofe to paint any thing from invention, when he could have the ob- jefts themfelves. The limbs of trees, which he collefted, would have made no inconfiderable wood-rick, and many an afs has been led into his painting-room.

He had tryed, if not *all* things, yet, *many* things, and held faſt thoſe which were right—but in one circumſtance he was ever wrong. In common with Vandyke, and a hoſt of other painters, he had two, and ſometimes three different points of ſight in the ſame picture. I have elſewhere * demonſtrated the falſity of this practice in a ſcientific view, and its ill effect in every ſenſe. A wholelength portrait of a child, with an horizon no higher than the ancles, gives one the idea of an infant as tall as a ſteeple, which is diſcordant and ridiculous—one of his prettieſt pictures was a child with ſuch an horizon.

The above obſervations on colouring apply equally to his portraits and hiſtories.

The firſt hiſtorical ſubject, in point of time, that occurs to me, is Garrick between

* In the Thirty Letters.

tween Tragedy and Comedy—which is a modernizing of Hercules between virtue and pleafure. It was painted long before the reformation in his colouring; but, notwithftanding that difadvantage, it is fo perfect in all other refpects, that it muft be confidered as one of the happieft efforts of his pencil.

It is not my intention to enter upon a criticifm, or even catalogue of his performances, or indeed to mention any picture; unlefs it contains fome peculiarity, by which a more correct judgement may be formed of his fkill, or the want of it. Suffice it then to fay, that there are trifling defects in moft of them, which an ordinary genius might have avoided; and tranfcendent beauties, which few, perhaps none, could have reached but himfelf. The *fketch* * of the infant Hercules

---

* I call it a fketch, becaufe it was evidently a ftudy for the great picture, but it was compleat in every

cules I have ever confidered as the firft production of his pencil, and the greateft effort of modern art.

He frequently painted hiftorical portraits—one of the beft is that of Mrs. Siddons in the character of the Tragic Mufe—it has grandeur in the conception and execution—but the fublimity of this picture is much abated by the abominable chair, which is fo ugly and difcordant, as to force our attention to fuch a fubordinate circumftance—nor is that the worft, for one of the odious knobs cuts the line of the arm, and fubftitutes a difagreeable break, where every thing fhould be broad and grand. I very much diflike the effect of the chair in the King's portrait at

the

every refpect. Surely one of the grandeft characters that ever mind conceived, or hand executed! If the reft of the figures had been only a woman or two, and in the fame ftyle, the infant would have kept its confequence, which is now loft amid a group of figures that offend probability, and deftroy the effect of the picture.

the Royal Academy: although it be the coronation chair, we fhould obferve, that when the King fat in it, the whole was richly covered—as a plain chair, it is fcarcely good enough for a country barber's fhop—where 1 heartily wifh it had been fent, before the imitation occurred, which has fo much hurt this capital performance.

In one of his early hiftorical portraits, the idea feems to be a reproach inftead of a compliment, he painted Lady Sarah Lennox as facrificing to the Graces. A little examination of the fubject, will, I believe, fhew that it was a wrong conception.

A poet once carried his verfes to a friend (fays Addifon, from whom I take the ftory) who returned them with advifing him " to facrifice to the *Graces*" —plainly infinuating, that he thought his poetry deftitute of elegance, and that he
fhould

fhould endeavour to propitiate the deities who were unfavourable to him—the application is obvious.

About the beginning of this century was a painter in Exeter called Gandy,* of whofe colóuring Sir Jofhua thought highly. I heard him fay, that on his return from Italy, when he was frefh from feeing the pictures of the Venetian School, he again looked at the works of Gandy, and that they had loft nothing in his eftimation.

It has been obferved, that Sir Jofhua was fhy of painting feet, and feldom ventured beyond the toe of a fhoe peeping out from a petticoat—there is fome reafon for this remark—but many things might

* There are many pictures of this artift in Exeter, and its neighbourhood. The portrait Sir Jofhua feemed moft to value, is in the Hall belonging to the College of Vicars in that city—but I have feen fome very much fuperior to it.

might be offered to excufe, though not
fufficient to defend the practice.

There are fewer drawings by this great
artift than by any other of eminence.
Perhaps, prevented by more important
occupations, or for want of early practice,
he might not poffefs the faculty of producing effect by chalks, wafhing, penning,
or any other of the numberlefs methods
by which drawings are made. The great
merit of which confifts of effect quickly
produced. This facility cannot be attained, however good our ideas may be,
without immenfe practice. Gainfborough
was for ever drawing, and had this facility; but there are not many proofs, that,
in this fenfe, Sir Jofhua drew at all.

His judgment of pictures differed from
connoiffeurs in general; was peculiar,
and his own. Very moderate ones (to
the common judge) he has fpoken highly
of; and very good ones (upon the ufual
principle

principle) he has much undervalued. His own collection (with fome illuftrious exceptions) and the little attention paid to R.˙ph's exhibition, feem to juftify this remark. Fifty quotations * from as many different authors will never make the Joconde of Leonardo da Vinci worth fifty pence—the fame may be faid of the Leda of Michael Angelo, and of many others which wanted other requifites to make them of value. But it fhould be obferved, that an artift frequently buys a picture for its poffeffing fomething that is of ufe to *him*, and which is undifcernable by the common eye—and this accounts for his having many pictures, the merit of which was only known to himfelf.

It was not apparent that Sir Jofhua was a fcholar, in the ufual acceptation of the

* In the catalogue were extracts, from a variety of writers, to fhew the excellence of fome of the pictures.

the word—but his converfation and writings fhewed a mind ftrongly tinctured
with modern literature and refinement.
There is much ingenuity and originality
in all his academic difcourfes—perhaps
there would have been more of both, if
he had dared to fhake off the fetters in
which long literary flavery has confined
us. Where he has done fo, as in his
Notes on Frefnoy, and his Eloge on
Gainfborough, it is evident that he could
think, and think juftly, for himfelf. His
ftyle is fimple and unaffected, and perfectly expreffive of his ideas, which, in
fact, is faying every thing. Thofe who
thought his difcourfes had been corrected
by Dr. Johnfon, were abfurd in the extreme. Sir Jofhua knew perfectly well
that Johnfon was the laft man in the
world for fuch a purpofe, and, befides,
muft be confident that he himfelf was
fully equal to the expreffion of his own
thoughts. Johnfon and Sir Jofhua, it is
true, were intimate friends, but they
were

were as unlike in every thing as two fenfible men could be. This matter admits
of proof—their writings bear not the leaft
refemblance to each other in fubject,
manner, or ftyle.

Whatever defects a critical eye might
find in his works, a microfcopic eye could
difcover none in his heart. If conftant
good-humour and benevolence, if the
abfence of every thing difagreeable, and
the prefence of every thing pleafant, be
recommendations for a companion, Sir
Jofhua had thefe accomplifhments. His
unfortunate deafnefs occafioned a practice
of loud fpeaking at his table, which to
thofe who were unufed to it was very
unpleafant;* but it was, notwithftanding,

* The greateft part of what is faid in company
is only good at the moment—if you are obliged to
repeat it, and with vehemence; what was before
important enough for the occafion, pretends to too
much, and becomes a mere nothing.

N

ing, the conftant refort of the firft people in England for rank and talents, by whom Sir Jofhua was efteemed and beloved— and this is the utmoft to which man can attain. The great, the wife, the inge- nious, and the good, ever confidered it as an honour to be known as the friends and intimates of Sir Jofhua Reynolds !*

With the fame freedom that I have fketched the characters of thofe two great painters, I will fet their merits *in oppo- fition* to each other—for the ufual word of *parallel* will not ferve the purpofe.

Sir Jofhua was always in the way of information and improvement, by con- ftantly affociating with men of talents and learning.

Gainfborough

* This fheet was in the prefs at the time Mr. Malone's confiderable work on the fame fubject was announced—fo that any agreement with, or difference from it, is perfectly accidental.

Gainfborough avoided the company of literary men, who were his averfion—he was better pleafed to give, than to receive information.

Sir J. (not becaufe he was deaf) wanted all idea and perception of mufic, being perfectly deftitute of ear.

G. had as correct an ear as poffible, and great enjoyment of exquifite inftrumental performance—vocal mufic he did not relifh.

Sir J. confidered hiftorical painting as the great point of perfection to which artifts fhould afpire, and was himfelf in the firft rank of excellence.

G. either wanted conception or tafte, to relifh hiftorical painting, which he always confidered as out of his way, and thought he fhould make himfelf ridiculous by attempting it.

Sir

Sir J. never painted a landſcape, except the two views from his villa at Rich-
mond—ſubjeĉts altogether improper for
a piĉture, and by no means happily executed—the little touches of landſcape
which he frequently introduced in the
back-ground of portraits were in a much
ſuperior ſtyle, and well calculated for the
effeĉt intended.

G. painted ſome hundreds of land-
ſcapes of different degrees of merit—
ſome, little better than waſhed drawings,
others very rich—but they all poſſeſſed
that freedom of pencilling which will for
ever make them valuable in the eye of an
artiſt.

Sir J. never painted cattle, ſhipping,
or other ſubordinate ſubjeĉts.

G. painted cattle of all denominations
very finely. He never pretended to the
correĉtneſs of rigging, &c. but I have

feen

feen fome general effects of fea, fea-coaft, and veffels, that have been truly mafterly.

Sir J. in portraits was different according to the æra of his practice—in his beft times his pictures poffeffed an elegance of defign—pictorefque draperies—beautiful difpofition of parts and circumftances; and certainly were greatly fuperior to thofe of all other artifts.

G. was always fure of a likenefs—not frequently happy in attitude or difpofition of parts. His pencilling was fometimes thin and hatchy, fometimes rich and full; but always poffeffing a facility of touch, which, as in his landfcapes, makes the worft of his pictures valuable.

Sir J. made very few drawings—it is natural to fuppofe that he made fome; but as I never faw any, they cannot be fuppofed to be numerous, nor can I fay any thing upon the fubject.

Of

Of Gainſborough, on the contrary, perhaps, there are more drawings exiſting than of any other artiſt, ancient or modern. I muſt have ſeen at leaſt a thouſand, not one of which but poſſeſſes merit, and ſome in a tranſcendent degree—two ſmall ones in ſlight tint, varniſhed, in the poſſeſſion of Mr. Baring of Exeter, are invaluable !

Sir J. as an author, wrote two or three papers in the Idler, ſome Notes for Johnſon's Edition of Shakeſpeare, and a few other incidental performances. His greateſt literary work are his Diſcourſes at the Royal Academy, which are replete with claſſical knowledge in his art—original obſervations—acute remarks on the works of others, and general taſte and diſcernment. In his Eloge on Gainſborough are traits of kindneſs and goodneſs of heart, exceedingly affecting to thoſe who knew the ſubject ! His Diſcourſes are collected and publiſhed together—they will

will be moſt valued by thoſe who are beſt qualified to judge of their excellence.

G. ſo far from writing, ſcarcely ever read a book—but, for a letter to an intimate friend, he had few equals, and no ſuperior. It was like his converſation, gay, lively—fluttering round ſubjects which he juſt touched, and away to another—expreſſing his thoughts with ſo little reſerve, that his correſpondents conſidering the letter as a part of their friend, had never the heart to burn it!

Sir Joſhua's character was moſt ſolid—Gainſborough's moſt lively—Sir J. wiſhed to reach the foundation of opinions. The ſwallow, in her airy courſe, never ſkimmed a ſurface ſo light as Gainſborough touched all ſubjects—that bird could not fear drowning more, than he dreaded deep diſquiſitions. Hitherto we have marked the difference of theſe great men. In one thing, and, I believe, in

one

one only they perfectly agreed—they each possessed a heart full-fraught with the warmest wishes for the advancement of the divine art they professed—of kindness to their friends—and general benevolence to men of merit, wherever found, and however distinguished.

Whether

Whether Genius be born, or acquired?

THOSE who hold the doctrine of " Poeta *nafcitur*," conceive human nature as
confifting of two parts, matter and fpirit;
and although each of thefe acts upon the
other, yet that they are two diftinct
things; for the body may be excited
to action by fenfation only, and the foul
may perform all its functions while the
body remains perfectly at reft.

By extending this principle, they fay,
that the mind may be weak while the
body is ftrong; or that the body may be
emaciated by difeafe, while the mind poffeffes all its vigour. Hence they confirm
the firft idea, that body and foul are independent of each other, and that the
latter may, and will remain, when the
former

former lives no more—but the certainty, or even poſſibility of a ſeparate exiſtence, makes no part of my ſubject.

Admitting the point to be eſtabliſhed, that man is a compound of a ſpiritual and corporeal nature, and that the two qualities, tho' united in him, are in themſelves diſtinct, we feel no difficulty of aſſigning all intellectual faculties to the ſoul only. Of courſe, genius is a property of the ſoul; and, together with all other modifications of intellect, perfectly independent of the body.

Of late, it has been thought that *Poeta fit*. It is circumſtances, ſay the profeſſors of this new doctrine, that determine our purſuits, our judgment, our apprehenſions, and that give genius or withhold it. A child juſt born may be made any thing you pleaſe—an orator, poet, painter, or muſician. If you wiſh that your ſon ſhould ſpeak like Cicero, write

like

like Homer, paint like Apelles, or compofe like Timotheus; fet the models before him which he is to imitate, keep
him intent on his fubject, put his thoughts
in the train they fhould go, and, if accidents do not interrupt their progrefs, they
will proceed onward to the goal, until
they fuccefsfully reach it.

The philofophers of the firft fect confider genius as infpiration—thofe of the
latter, as imitation. If nature has denied
you genius, fay the former, you can never attain it—if you wifh to be a genius,
fay the latter, the means are in your own
power.

Upon the prefumption that this is the
true ftate of the queftion, we will examine whether the old or the new doctrine agrees beft with the facts which hiftory furnifhes relating to men of genius,
and how far our daily experience will
lead us to adopt one or the other.

Since

Since the exiftence of hiftory, not more than two or three poets are recorded to be of the firft clafs—perhaps only one who is *univerfally* allowed to be in the very firft rank. Few are the painters and ftatuaries of antiquity whofe works have defcended to the prefent times. The fame may be faid of architects and profeffors of the liberal arts and fciences in general. As fame is " the univerfal paffion," all may be fuppofed to covet the enjoyment of it; but fo very few poffeffing their wifh—which is the moft natural fuppofition, that the productions of genius depend upon our own power, or upon fomething which is beyond our command or attainment ?

If I rightly underftand the modern doctrine, it afferts, that if you defire to make two children artifts in the fame profeffion, and one proves deficient and and the other excellent; the difference does not arife from the children, but their
mode

mode of treatment—that certain circumftances put the good artift in the way of
becoming excellent, and different circumftances prevented the other from improvement; but if you had applied the
treatment which the ingenious artift received, to the other, then their talents
would have been reverfed. If you fay,
that to the beft of your ability you gave
to each equal opportunities of information; you are told, that the furnifhing
the mind with ideas depends upon a
thoufand niceties, which will not admit
of variation, and although your intention
was good, it was not executed. As this
feems to fhew that the affair is not in our
own power, we may prefume it to be in
other hands.

In thofe things which depend upon
precept or example, we always perceive
the force of early inftruction and cuftom.
A family educated in the principles of the
Church of England, or in thofe which

diffent

diffent from it, generally continues in the same perfuafion. Children, which are early accuftomed to virtuous and moral precepts, are undoubtedly more likely to become good members of fociety than if their education had been neglected. Thofe who in their infancy are taught the perfonal graces, have the eafieft carriage. In thefe inftances, and many others, we confefs the full force of external impreffions, tho' we cannot fo readily affent to their power of producing genius. But admitting, for a moment, that genius is not innate, yet if the means for acquiring it be not in our power, it is of very little fignification to the argument, whether a child is *born* with that propenfity to poetry, painting, or mufic, which we call genius, or whether he afterwards imbibes it: whether it be a property of the foul, or a quality of the body.

That thefe means are not in our power, is evident, from paft experience, and prefent

fent obfervation : if you cannot tell how to produce another Homer, Apelles, or Timotheus; fhould fuch beings again exift, it muft depend upon fomething which does not belong to our efforts, and is beyond our knowledge.

Thofe who conceive genius to be no-thing but a *tafte* for the arts, very much under-rate its importance. Genius, in-deed, poffeffes this tafte, but its effence is a *creative* power to " body forth the fhapes of things unknown, and give to aery nothing a local habitation and a name." Whoever read the original paf-fage without that thrill of delight always attendant on fublime expreffions? Who, but earneftly wifhed to equal its force and beauty? But yet, out of the millions of men who have peopled this globe in long fucceffion, not one, no, *not one* ever did, perhaps, ever could conceive, and utter this idea in terms equally fublime!

If

If genius could be acquired, it feems unaccountable that we have not another Shakefpeare—nay, a poet as much his fuperior as he is above all others; for why fhould we ftop, when by continual exertion we may at laft afcend a height to look down on the top of Helicon? —*feriens fidera vertice.*

I have already hinted, that genius muft not be miftaken for tafte to relifh the productions of others, or ability to imitate them. One half the world might be taught to copy high-finifhed drawings, as that kind of talent is by no means unufual. To produce effect with little trouble can only be attained by long practice, which induces facility. But original conceptions, and new arrangements of thofe forms and circumftances of which pictures are compofed, are the property of genius alone: they do not depend upon imitation, and can never be taught.

Perhaps

Perhaps the fubject may be farther il-
luftrated by fome obfervations with which
mufic will furnifh us.

Some perfons are born without ear,
which no art can create. Let them hear
mufic ever fo often, let thofe who wifh
to give, and thofe who wifh to acquire
this fenfation, exert their utmoft efforts
—it is in vain—earlefs they were, and
fo they will remain to the laft moment
of their lives.

Thofe who have an ear for mufic may
become proficients in that art, in proportion to their ability—they may fing, or
perform on an inftrument, and proceed
in excellence, according to the extent of
their practice, or opportunity for improvement—but all this is far fhort of
genius. Perhaps, twenty perfons have
an ear for one that wants it; but not one
performer in a hundred has genius to
create mufic of his own—the greater

O   number

number of practical muficians are as far
from the *invention* of melody, as if they
had never heard, or touched an inftrument; and, what makes altogether for
the fupport of the firft opinion, notwithftanding their utmoft wifhes and inceffant
endeavours, it is not in the power of human art to give them this invention.

Should thofe unacquainted with mufic,
fay, that the want of fuccefs is becaufe
the proper means have not been tried—I
can only reply, that no means which the
knowledge and practice of the art can
furnifh, ever fucceeded to give ear and
genius where nature had denied them;
and it feems hard to fuppofe that perfons
ignorant of the fcience fhould poffefs a
fecret denied to profeffors.

This is intended as a fair enquiry into
the different merit of the two opinions,
and the refult is undoubtedly in favour of
the firft. The caufe, or confequence of
genius

genius not depending on ourfelves, fortunately makes no part of my fubject, for
I confefs myfelf ignorant of the firft ftep
towards fo abftrufe an inveftigation. I
only wifhed to fhew, and in as few words
as poffible, that genius was fomething
not mechanical; that it is given, not acquired; and whether it be corporeal or
immaterial, whether making part of our
firft exiftence, or afterwards imbibed, yet
that it is not in the power of man to
give, or take it away.

The difference of opinion on this fubject may be owing to the not diftinguifhing between genius and talents. At firft
fight they may appear the fame, but upon
examination we fhall difcover more than
a fhade of diftinction. A man of genius
muft have talents, but talents are poffeffed by many, without it. Genius, tho'
poffeffing talents, has not always the
power of fhewing them, for want of
mechanical facility; and talents are fre-

O 2   quently

quently exercifed with fo much excellence, as to be miftaken for genius. However paradoxical this may appear, all difficulty vanifhes, by confidering that the charaćteriftic of genius is *invention, a creation of fomething not before exifting;* to which talents make no pretence: and although talents and genius are fometimes united, yet they are in their nature diftinćt.

An aćtor may poffefs every propriety of fpeaking and aćtion without the ability of writing a play, in which cafe, he has talents only: but, if he add to his performance the invention of a dramatic fable, he has then talents and genius.

A mufician may be an exquifite performer without having one mufical idea of his own—he has talents: but if he poffefs a fund of original melody, he has genius; for harmony already exifts independent of invention, and that fucceffion

of

of chords, and ſtructure of parts, termed compoſition, are the fruit of information and practice: by theſe we judge of his *ſkill*, but we eſtimate the *invention* of a compoſer from his melody.

As talents are commonly miſtaken for genius, and are the conſequence of cultivation, it is natural to give the ſame origin to both: but let the qualities of each be conſidered, and they will appear, as from the above inſtances, to be different things, and to ariſe from different ſources.

A man of talents has a much fairer proſpect of good fortune than a man of genius. There are few inſtances of talents being neglected, and fewer ſtill of genius being encouraged. The world is a perfect judge of talents, but thoroughly ignorant of genius. Any art already known, if carried to a greater height, is at once rewarded; but the new crea-

tions

tions of genius are not at firft underftood,
and there muft be fo many repetitions of
the effect before it is felt, that moft
commonly death fteps in between genius and its fame. This idea is farther
purfued in another place.*

I make a *diftinction* between talents
and genius, but it muft not be imagined
that I wifh to fet them at variance; for
the nearer talents can be brought to re-
femble genius, the ftronger will be their
effect; and the more genius poffeffes the
ability of making its creations manifeft,
the lefs will its powers be confined to
that mind in which they were originally
conceived.

* In the Thirtieth Letter.

The

The Venetian, French Captain, and Prieſt.

WHEN Buonaparte invaded the Duchy of Milan, one of his advanced parties, not ſtrictly attentive to the bounds of territories, encroached upon the State of Venice. The owner of a villa in the neighbourhood, perceiving a band of foreign ſoldiers marching up the avenue, thought it prudent to advance half-way to meet them. The Captain, in a few words, acquainted him, that they were troops of the new Republic, meant no offence to that of Venice, and would quit the territory immediately—" Not before you have dined," replied the gentleman, " enter the houſe with me—your men ſhall be entertained in Freſco."

O 4　　　　During

During the dinner, the difcourfe turned on the great events of the prefent times.

" Vivent les Republiques!" fays the Captain, filling his glafs—

" Vive la Republique !" faid the Venetian.

C. Do you mean a flight to France, Signor ?

V. I thought if the meaning of an expreffion was doubtful, a Frenchman always underftood it for his advantage. I drank fuccefs, Monfieur, to the Republic of France—our own Republic is funk too low to be worth a glafs of wine, or even a wifh for its profperity.

C. Impoffible ! all Republics, becaufe they are fo, muft flourifh.

V.

V. *Our* time is paſt—we grew—came to maturity, and are now decayed.

C. A Republic decay! kings, tyrants, deſpots, cauſe the ruin of countries; but where freedom is eſtabliſhed—

V. Ha, ha, ha!—and ſo you really think that a republican government produces freedom?

C. Can you doubt it? A very few years ago, we in France were all ſlaves—now, thank Heaven—no—thank our own efforts—we are free!

V. We Venetians think differently—during the monarchy of France, all looked up to you as the great, the happy nation of Europe—now we think you miſerable ſlaves, like ourſelves.

C. Slaves!—explain yourſelf—

V.

V. Readily. Nothing flatters the imagination more than the idea of liberty —but let us not feek it where the fearch muft be vain. *Abfolute* liberty cannot exift in focial life. If liberty be better than every thing elfe, give up fociety, and rove the woods as a favage.

C. What! is there no liberty con-fiftent with fociety?

V. Yes—but the *abfolute* liberty you contend for, is not. It is the firft prin-ciple of government to abridge liberty.

C. Allowing it; there is a difference in governments—under fome you have a certain degree of liberty; under others, you have lefs; but under an abfolute prince you have none at all.

V. Say rather, that under a mixed monarchy, you have a little tyranny; under an unlimited monarch, you have
more;

more; but in a Republic, the unhappy
citizen, flattered with the *idea* of liberty,
is moſt enſlaved, and with the additional
mortification, that he is ſo by perſons no
greater than himſelf. As the old lion,
in the fable, juſtly remarked, the kick
of an aſs is not only pain, but indignity.

C. You ſpeak an odd language for a
Republican—but, now I recollect, you
are governed by an Ariſtocracy.

V. I ſpoke of the different forms of
government in general, without any particular application. But you are governed
by an Ariſtocracy as much as we are—
notwithſtanding your averſion to the term
Ariſtocrat. In fact, a pure Republic is
no government at all—there muſt be perſons either naturally or artificially elevated to manage the buſineſs of the ſtate,
and theſe perſons are an Ariſtocracy. In
Venice, the nobles are born our governors; in France, you elevate from your
own

own rank the perfons who govern—the difference to the people is nothing.

C. There is furely *this* difference—the power of our rulers is only for a time—yours is for life.

V. It feems to be fo, but it is a diftinction, without a difference, as far as the people are concerned. In Venice the whole body of nobles furnifhes the officers of government; we know their number and their character, fo that we are enabled to direct an oppofition, if neceffary, when, and how we pleafe. In France there is an indefinite number of perfons, who, by good-fortune, intrigue, bribery, by talents, and fome even by vices, ftand forward in your Republic as the nobles do in ours—and thefe govern your country—

C. In a pure Republic, like ours, all places are open to all perfons—in yours,

yours, no one can fucceed that is not a noble.

V. This, which you mention as an advantage, is certainly a dire misfortune. At the commencement of your revolution, many different parties were ftriving for their own purpofes, to which the public good was fubfervient—the party in power facrificed the others, and were in turn deftroyed by their fucceffors. As you in the beginning declared, that all were equal, it gave a pretence to every individual to govern the ftate, and by his elevation to contradict your principle—and this muft ever be the cafe. I can eafily conceive that the people may be aggrieved under any government. When they feel themfelves oppreffed, it is natural to wifh for a change, and, if poffible, effect it. If there were no Republics in Europe, a country might be excufed for blundering into a conftitution which looks fo fpecioufly; but as there

are

are fo many, why not firft examine whether they are the abodes of liberty? From
their hiftory, alfo, it would be found,
that they begun upon your principle, but
could not continue their exiftence until
another was adopted. Venice, Genoa,
and Holland, were obliged to have a
Chief Magiftrate, who at leaft *reprefented*
a Sovereign—the new Republic of America could not act without a Prefident,
nor could you without a Directory. In
fact, a kingly government is the moft
natural of all others, and although people
upon ill-ufage may fly from it with fury,
like a pendulum fwung violently, yet,
every vibration brings it nearer and nearer
to the centre, where, at laft, it naturally
refts. The French Republic is at prefent paffing furioufly through this centre
of vibration, but unlefs there is fome new
force to continue the motion, it muft
ceafe at laft. England was once precifely
in the fame fituation, and ended her vibration in monarchy.

C.

C. Our conftitution is now fixed—
our Cinq-Vir can *execute* our laws, but
cannot infringe them—they have the neceffary fplendour of a fovereign without
his power to hurt.

V. This is all very good—but why
did you change your old government?

C. To be free.

V. Good again—but even freedom
itfelf is of no value if it does not procure
happinefs. Under the monarchy, a powerful army (affembled without force) was
at your command; the third commerce
of Europe was yours; and you had the
fecond fleet; money, at leaft to individuals, was in plenty; arts and fciences
flourifhed; your people increafed, and
every thing was fo pleafant and comfortable about you, that foreigners preferred a
refidence in France to any other country.
But fince you have been a Republic, the
reverfe

reverfe has taken place : your commerce, fleet, and money, are not merely dimi- nifhed, but almoft annihilated ; you have wantonly thrown away two millions of lives, which you forced into your army, and France is confidered no longer the feat of elegant pleafure, but the abode of vulgarity, poverty, and wretchednefs.

C. Whenever there is a ftruggle for liberty it muft coft fomething ; it may coft much, but the prize, when obtained, is invaluable !

V. Gold may be bought too dear—but *are* you free after all ? We think, not. Your lives and property are lefs fecure than under your kings ; and, inftead of having liberty of fpeech and action, you are more watched than we are by our in- quifition. Be not deceived—the ftate may be free, and yet individuals may be flaves. In the ecclefiaftical territories, governed by the moft abfolute of princes,

is

is more liberty than is to be found in all the Republics of Europe—fo, in compliment to the Red-cap Goddefs wherever found (filling his glafs) *Viva il Padre fantiffimo!*

Viva, viva! faid the Confeffor of the Houfehold, entering with prieftly freedom—*viva il Padre fantiffimo!* lifting up his eyes with true devotion, and emptying his glafs. The French Captain felt fome difficulties—as a national officer he could not drink the Pope's health; but as a gueft in a houfe, where he had been civilly treated, fome remains of the old French politeffe prompted him to dribble a little wine into his glafs, which he fipped in filence.

V. I fee you do not join us cordially; but if you really loved freedom, you would not object to its patron.

P   C.

C. You know that our civil and religious reformation have kept pace together—when we abolifhed our old government we deftroyed our church eftablifhments—

Here the Prieft exclaimed—

P. Deftroy church eftablifhments! How can you expect a bleffing upon your undertaking when you ftop the fource of it?

C. We expect no bleffing—we only defire fuccefs, and that we fhall procure by our invincible troops.

P. Santa Maria!

C. Pray, my good father, can you give me a fingle inftance of a bleffing being obtained in confequence of afking it, or any petition you have preferred to Heaven, being granted?

P.

P. We hope for the beſt—it is our buſineſs to pray—but to grant, is in other hands.

V. Well anſwered, Padre—It is ſaid (ſpeaking to the Captain) that you have diſcarded religion, but as that is ſo much greater than your other follies, I never until now believed it. Let us ſuppoſe that you could by a law aboliſh all the forms of religion, would it then be eradicated from hearts where it was ſo early implanted? If you could root it out, do you not leave a vacancy that nothing elſe can ſupply? Are there not numberleſs duties which are termed, of imperfect obligation, that no laws can reach, and which can only be enforced by religion?

C. Theſe points are rather out of a ſoldier's line of life, to whom it is more natural to cut knots than to untie them—however, it is my inclination, as well as my duty, to defend my country and li-

berty.

berty. When we firſt began to think,
which deſpotiſm ſo long prevented, we
ſoon perceived that ſuperſtition was the
right hand of tyranny—that it was religion run mad, and that to deſtroy ſuperſtition for ever we muſt begin our attack
at the ſource. We did ſo, and preſently
found that religion was leſs founded on
truth than on cuſtom, and that cuſtom
had produced prejudice in its favour—

P. What dreadful !—

C. That all the benefit ſuppoſed to
be derived from religion, was attainable
in a greater degree by the practice of
virtue—

P. Which cannot—

C. ——but that even virtue could
not exiſt without liberty, therefore we
made liberty our firſt point, in expecta-
tion

tion that " all the reſt," as my impatient Padre would ſay, " ſhould be added."

P. If I am impatient, excuſe me—but is it for your *worldly* intereſt to reject the only comfort in affliction?

C. We either ſeek conſolation by bearing our misfortunes like men, or braving them as heroes. If we are to die, we do not aſk a Prieſt to frighten us day after day in a long interval between doom and execution, or ſickneſs and death; but give up our lives with reſolution, in many inſtances with triumph, the inſtant we know that our fate is determined.

P. All this does for the preſent moment, but—think of the future!

C. That certainly makes no part of the character of my countrymen—however, to oblige you, I will conſider it. The future is not in our power—if our

ſins

fins have made us worthy of punifhment, we fhall certainly receive it—you cannot be fo foolifh to imagine, that by a few repentant words we fhall alter eternal decrees. Befides, we have difcarded the doctrine of a future ftate. Suppofing it to exift, our chance for happinefs is as good as yours.

P. Thofe who have ftrayed but little from the fold may be brought back again to it; but what can recover the fheep that is totally loft? Son, if you do not believe, you cannot be faved!

C. Surely, my good Padre, if I have a foul, it does not ceafe to exift becaufe I *difbelieve* its exiftence—and although I may be fo blind, fo foolifh, or fo obfti-nate, as to deny a future ftate, yet if there *be* fuch a ftate, I fhall, I muft par-take of it as well as your reverence, and be happy or miferable according to my actions, not my belief.

V.

V. Your conftitution and religion are both of a piece—one would not have been perfect without the other.

C. We think fo—whereas *your* conftitution and religion are at variance—a Republic under the denomination of prieft-craft is only free by halves—but hark! the drum beats—Signor, farewell!—Padre, adieu! perhaps the time is not far remote when truth will demolifh all our private opinions, and fpread, like the arms of the Republic, over the face of the earth!

V. He is gone off like a cannon—

P. The joy of the wicked is but for a moment. Son, we have both finned in liftening to this French Atheift—let us forget what we have heard, and go to Vefpers.

The

The Bard.

POETRY, to deferve our attention, muft either be regular and faultlefs; or it muft be irregularly great, and poffefs tranfcendent beauties, to attone for eminent defects. The moderns are chiefly of the former character, and the ancients of the latter.

It by no means follows from this diftinction, that the moderns are never fublime, or the ancients never regular and equal; but the early age of fociety (which is the ancient, let it happen at any period) is moft favourable to Genius, and the advanced ftate of mankind to Tafte. It was in our own times that Gray writ the Ode which makes my prefent fubject —it is entitled The Bard, and poffeffes

much

much of the ancient fire combined with modern tafte.

Perhaps it is this combination which weakens the fublimity of the poem; for in this refpect it is very inferior to Dryden's Alexander's Feaft: but when the regularity of the ftructure is confidered, and the exquifite polifh with which the whole is finifhed, we ought to confider it as one of the moft perfect productions of our time. This perfection will plainly appear upon a curfory review (for I mean no more) of its fable—ftructure—verfification—fentiments—and general effect.

Story.

A fmall event is fufficient for an ode, but yet there fhould be *fome* event. Compare the odes which are dramatic, to thofe which are only fentimental, and the fuperior effect of ftory will be very apparent. Even the Elegy in the Country Church-

Church-yard, beautiful as it is, depends as much upon the fcenery, and the little incident which makes its fable, as upon the fentiment and poetry—we have the latter in other pieces of the fame poet, which wanting the former, fail of exciting our feelings, and commanding our attention.

This Poem has incident fufficient to make it interefting, but not enough to be oppreffed by adventure. It is not only interefting, but pictorefque, in an eminent degree—an old Bard fitting on the edge of a precipice that overhangs a torrent, addreffing his prophetic ftrains to a king who defcends a mountain at the head of his army, is a fubject as proper for painting as poetry. The fcenery is farther enriched by ideal perfonages, and -romantic fplendour is added to natural magnificence. The conducting of the ftory is altogether epic—it begins in the midft of a great incident—it informs of

all

all that is neceſſary to be known preceding—it looks into futurity, and ends triumphantly. The incidents of the Engliſh Hiſtory, which it was neceſſary to introduce, although ſlightly touched, yet it is done " with a maſter's hand and poet's fire."

The Structure

Is a regular pindaric, What the critics term the ode, epode, and antiſtrophe, are each divided into three parts; every line of the ode has preciſely the ſame number of ſyllables with the correſponding line of the epode and antiſtrophe—the rhymes are in the ſame places, and the fifteenth and ſeventeenth lines of the third ſtanza of the ode, having a word in the middle which rhymes with one at the end, are anſwered by lines of the ſame ſtructure in the third ſtanzas of the epode and antiſtrophe. If there be any merit in this regularity, the poem has the fulleſt claim

to

to it—the difficulty was great, and it is happily vanquiſhed.

The Verſification

Is various—much ſtudied, and if arti-ficial, it is at leaſt eaſy, flowing, and full of dignity.

Perhaps, the moſt exceptionable line is the firſt, in which is the appearance of an affected alliteration. If this affectation be once ſuſpected, we rather withhold our fancy than indulge it, and read with caution inſtead of enjoyment.

The Sentiments

Are characteriſtic of the perſonages who ſpeak in this dramatic ode—the Bard is deeply impreſſed with ſorrow for the loſs of his companions, and pours forth his imprecations on the tyrant who had taken their lives. The ghoſts of the
murdered

murdered bards exprefs their prophetic curfes in the fpirit of the Northern Scalds, of whofe works Mr. Gray was an admirer. Thefe, to ufe an expreffion of the authors, are " thoughts that breathe, and words that burn." The breaking off from the ghofts to the vifion of the bard, (to whofe imagination are prefented the great poets that are to flourifh in future ages) is truly poetical; it has the farther ufe of reconciling him to his fate, and making him triumph in that death which was inevitable.

Effect.

The effect of a pindaric ode (and indeed of all fublime writing) is to produce that elevation of foul, which, while we read, feems to add increafe of Being.

The firft line commands our attention, and we feel ourfelves expanding as the poem advances, which never finks

fo

fo low as mediocrity; and if no particular paffage can be quoted as the higheft pitch of fublimity, yet the whole together has a degree of perfection that has feldom been attained, and perhaps never exceeded by any poet ancient or modern.

The Ghost.

IT was shrewdly remarked by Voltaire, that the early stages of society are the times for prodigies—Scotland was not civilized when Macbeth met the Witches; nor was Rome, when Curtius leaped into the Gulph. People of weak intellects, have, at all times, believed in apparitions. It is unnecessary now to say, that stories of Ghosts are mistakes or impositions, and that they might always be detected, if people had ingenuity to discover the trick, or courage enough to search out the cause of their fright:

In all relations of this kind there is manifestly an endeavour to make the event as supernatural, wonderful, and as well-attested as possible, to prevent the suspi-

cion

cion of trick, and to cut off all objections which might be made to its credibility. I am about to comply with the eſtabliſhed cuſtom, and ſhall relate a ſtory of a Ghoſt, which, I will be bold to ſay, has the ſtrongeſt circumſtances of the wonderful, the ſupernatural, and the well-atteſted, of any upon record. The ſtory, as yet, only lives in tradition, but it is much too good to be loſt.

At a town in the weſt of England was held a club of twenty-four people, which aſſembled once a week to drink punch, ſmoke tobacco, and talk politics. Like Rubens's Academy at Antwerp, each member had his peculiar chair, and the Preſident's was more exalted than the reſt. One of the members had been in a dying ſtate for ſome time ; of courſe, his chair, while he was abſent, remained vacant.

The club being met on their uſual night, enquiries were naturally made after
their

their affociate. As he lived in the adjoining houfe, a particular friend went
himfelf to enquire for him, and returned
with the difmal tidings that he could not
poffibly furvive the night. This threw
a gloom on the company, and all efforts
to turn the converfation from the fad fubject before them were ineffectual.

About midnight, (the time, by long
prefcription, appropriated for the walking of fpectres) the door opened—and
the Form, in white, of the dying, or rather of the dead man, walked into the
room, and took his feat in the accuftomed
chair—there he remained in filence, and
in filence was he gazed at. The apparition continued a fufficient time in the
chair to affure all prefent of the reality of
the vifion; at length, he arofe and ftalked
towards the door, which he opened, as if
living—went out, and then fhut the door
after him.—

Q   After

After a long paufe, fome one at laft had the refolution to fay,' " if only *one* of us had feen this, he would not have been believed, but it is impoffible that fo many perfons can be deceived."

The company, by degrees, recovered their fpeech; and the whole converfation, as may be imagined, was upon the dreadful object which had engaged their attention. They broke up, and went home.

In the morning, enquiry was made after their fick friend—it was anfwered by an account of his death, which happened nearly at the time of his appearing in the club. There could be little doubt before, but now nothing could be more certain than the reality of the apparition, which had been feen by fo many perfons together.

It is needlefs to fay, that fuch a ftory fpread over the country, and found credit

even

even from infidels : for in this cafe, all
reafoning became fuperfluous, when oppofed to a plain fact attefted by three and
twenty witneffes. To affert the doctrine
of the fixed laws of nature was ridiculous, when there were fo many people of
· credit to prove that they might be un-
fixed.

Years rolled on—the ftory ceafed to
engage attention, and it was forgotten,
unlefs when occafionally produced to
filence an unbeliever.

One of the club was an apothecary.
In the courfe of his practice he was called
to an old woman, whofe profeffion was
attending on fick perfons. She told him,
that fhe could leave the world with
a quiet confcience but for one thing
which lay on her mind—" Do you not
" remember Mr. *** whofe Ghoft has
" been fo much talked of? I was his
" nurfe. The night he died I left the

Q 2 " room

" room for fomething I wanted—I am
" fure I had not been abfent long; but
" at my return I found the bed without
" my patient. He was delirious, and I
" feared that he had thrown himfelf out
" of the window. I was fo frighted
" that I had no power no ftir; but after
" fome time, to my great aftonifhment,
" he entered the room fhivering, and his
" teeth chattering—laid down on the
" bed, and died. Confidering myfelf as
" the caufe of his death, I kept this a
" fecret, for fear of what might be done
" to me. Tho' I could contradict all the
" ftory of the Ghoft, I dared not to do
" it. I knew by what had happened
" that it was *he himfelf* who had been
" in the club-room (perhaps recollecting
" that it was the night of meeting) but
" I hope God, and the poor gentleman's
" friends will forgive me, and I fhall die
" contented !"

On Gentlemen-Artifts.

To attain excellence in the arts is the lot of very few profeffors, who have fpent their lives in the purfuit.

Gainfborough, after a clofe application to painting for fifty years, faid on his death-bed—" I am but juft *beginning* to do fomething, and my life is gone!" I could repeat expreffions of architects, fculptors, and muficians, grown old in the ftudy of their profeffions, to the fame purpofe; from whence we may conclude, that the ufual term of the duration of our faculties, is not fufficient to attain that perfection to which genius afpires.

This truth being admitted, for it cannot be denied, what fhall we fay to thofe

Q 3 peremptory

peremptory judgments which are paſſed upon the works of genius by perſons who never had, nor, perhaps, could have, a thought upon the ſubject? In any other caſe we ſhould judge them raſh and preſumptuous. No man, who is unacquainted with the common profeſſions and trades, ever pretends to know any thing about them—but every man fancies he can be an architect, painter, or muſician, with ſimply ſaying, like the Elector of Brandenburg—" I will be a King!" Every one feels himſelf equal to the deſigning and building a houſe—very few who do not think they might, if they choſe it, be painters—and what numbers of dilettanti are there, who, becauſe they poſſeſs ear, and perhaps a taſte for muſic, fancy they can compoſe?

Should theſe ſoi-diſant Artiſts exhibit proofs of their ſkill, it is natural to imagine, that their impotent attempts would only be deſpiſed, and make them ridiculous

lous—juſt the reverſe—their works are moſt favourably received—what they may poſſibly want in ſkill, ſay the public, they poſſeſs in taſte, and a natural taſte is every' thing.

I will leave it to the architects to ex-preſs their feelings in finding their plans rejected, and deſigns of theſe *taſty* per-ſons ſubſtituted for them; or; what is worſe, having their plans corrected by them, becauſe then there is ſuch a mix-ture of ignorance and ſcience, that we cannot always ſeparate the alloy from the gold. I will leave it to the painters to fret at the criticiſm of the gentlemen-ar-tiſts, and their being obliged to abandon their own conceptions to ſubſtitute the ideas of thoſe, who, on this ſubject, can-not think at all—but, I will make a few obſervations on the gentlemen-muſicians, as being more in my province, and which, indeed, was the occaſion of this ſhort eſſay.

Q 4   To

To perfons who have no ear, nor, of courfe, any real pleafure from mufic, this fubject muft feem to be ridiculous, from my confidering it, in any refpect, important—it is intended for thofe of another defcription.

The gentlemen-muficians may be divided into two claffes—the cultivators of performance, and compofition; to which may be added, thofe who unite both.

Nothing is more certain than that a great portion of time muft be applied to the practice of an inftrument before we can attain the rank of even a tolerable performer—to thofe who have other purfuits, this would be an unprofitable employment; it would be time mifpent, and cannot be afforded—from this confideration alone, there is a prefumption, that a perfon, not of the mufical profeffion, cannot have attained excellence on any inftrument, notwithftanding fome illuftrious

trious exceptions. How many a concert is fpoiled by gentlemen whofe tafte is to fupply their deficiency of practice and knowledge? However, although our ears are offended at the inftant, the affair is foon over, and we think no more of it —but this cannot be faid of the gentle-men-compofers.

Thefe, for the moft part, employ their talents in vocal mufic. If they are members of a Cathedral Church, they try their hand at a chant, and then boldly venture upon an anthem. Should it bear fome abortive refemblance to air and harmony, it is immediately confidered as a prodigy, and the works of Croft and Greene muft give way to the tafty production; which is fpread about the kingdom, that our church-mufic may be univerfally improved.

Others amufe themfelves in making a fucceffion of chords and call them Glees, which

which do the fame mifchief in concerts
and mufical parties, as the works of the
reverend compofers do in the church—
that is, they exclude real mufic, and
produce firft an endurance, and then a
liking of its oppofite.

It is my love to the arts, and refpect
to their profeffors, that call forth thefe
animadverfions. To thofe who are placed
by nature or fortune in a ftation of life
that makes the trouble of thefe acquire-
ments unneceffary, and the pretenfions to
them ridiculous, let me apply this fhort
ftory.—When Commodore Anfon was at
Canton, the officers of the Centurion had
a ball upon fome court holiday—while
they were dancing, a Chinefe, who very
quietly furveyed the operation, faid foftly
to one of the party—" Why don't you
let your fervants do this for you ?"

Permit me to add—that, though mufic
has its foundation in nature, the whole
of

of the fuperftructure is art—that much application is neceffary before knowledge will be acquired—and that no fubftitute for continual practice can produce facility. Previous to the firft ftep, nature muft have beftowed a talent for the invention of melody; but if this talent be not directed by the knowledge of compofition, and that knowledge continually exercifed, the talent had better have remained always " hidden in a napkin."

Coincidences.

Coincidences.

IN the laſt century, when aſtrology flou-
riſhed, it was uſual to remark a coincidence of days and circumſtances. The
unenlightened mind has a ſtrong propenſity to ſuch fancies, which adminiſter real
joy, or ſorrow, according to the nature
of the ſubject. Superſtition eaſily gives
a religious turn to them, and ſuch accidental concurrences are brought as proofs
of the ſuperintending care of providence,
in preference to the general arrangement
of cauſes and events.

The 3d of September was a day particularly ominous to Oliver Cromwell—
two or three of his battles were fought
and won upon that day, which, I think,
was alſo the day of his death.

De

De Foe, ſtrongly tinctured with ſuperſtition, in the true ſpirit of the times,
gives ominous days to Robinſon Cruſoe,
who had a variety of events which fell
out on the 23d of September.

It did not eſcape the obſervation of
Aubrey, that Alexander the Great was
born on the 6th of April—conquered
Darius—won a great victory at ſea—and
died on the ſame day of the ſame month.
In his Miſcellanies is a precious collection of ſuch inſtances.

An author, in the year 1736, publiſhed a pamphlet, called Numerus In-
fauſtus, or a ſhort View of the unfortunate Reigns of William 2—Henry 2—
Edward 2—Richard 2—Charles 2—and
James 2. This book came out in tem-
pore fauſto, for the Reign of George 2
could not properly have been added to
the catalogue.

In

In 1733, two hundred and four Members of the Houſe of Commons voted againſt the Exciſe Bill, 8 of them made ſpeeches againſt it. Theſe two numbers of 8 and 204 occaſioned the following remark

1	-	-	-	-	1
2	-	-	-	-	4
3	-	-	-	-	9
4	-	-	-	-	16
5	-	-	-	-	25
6	-	-	-	-	36
7	-	-	-	-	49
8	-	-	-	-	64
					204

The ſquare of each number, from 1 to 8 incluſive, makes united, the ſum of 204. This I conſider as the moſt ingenious of all thoſe conceits. But yet another occurs, which is alſo of the firſt conſideration—the famous number of the beaſt, 666,

666, ·that has puzzled fo many divine arithmeticians, is thus explained by the Rev. Mr. Vivian.

L	-	-	-	-	50
V	-	-	-	-	5
D	-	-	-	-	500
O	-	-	-	-	0
V	-	-	-	-	5
I	-	-	-	-	1
C	-	-	-	-	100
V	-	-	-	-	5
S	-	-	-	-	0
					———
					666
					———

This beaft has now " received his deadly wound."

There was a time, and that not very remote, when 45 was extolled beyond any other affemblage of numerals which art could invent. The coincidences with ancient and modern events made the fub-ject

ject of some paragraphs in every news-
paper—sometimes it was *numerus in-
fauſtus.* One man swore that he would
eat 45 pound of beef-steaks—another
that he would drink 45 pots of porter;
but they both died before the glorious
purpose could be accomplished—perhaps,
neither gluttony nor drunkenness were
the motives to this excess, but an ambi-
tion to be connected with 45.

Whoever might be the worse, to John
Wilkes himself this was a lucky number
—almoſt every article of life poured in
upon him in forty fives—among the reſt
I recollect 45 dozen of claret, and 45
dozen of candles, from an Alderman of
the name of White—this laſt gave occaſion to a humourous ballad, ending

> —— my muſe I no longer will dandle,
> So I wiſh you good night
> Mr. Alderman White
> With your 45 dozen of candle.

Very

Very lately, in a newſpaper, was the following article. " We left Falmouth " the 7th of Auguſt, 1794—nothing ma- " terial occurred until the 23d, on which " day we do in general look for ſucceſs, " as all our captures have been made on " the 23d." (Letter from an officer of the Flora, who I preſume had read Ro- binſoe Cruſoe). I heartily wiſh this ho- neſt gentleman may take a good French prize the 23d of every month as long as the war laſts !

I am ſo truly ſorry for the following coincidences, (taken from a newſpaper,) that I ſhall give them ſimply, without remark—

On the 21ſt of April, 1770, Louis XVI. was married.

———— 21ſt of June, 1770, was the Fête when 1500 perſons were tram- pled to death.

On

R

On the 21ſt of Jan. 1782, Fête for the birth of the Dauphin.

———— 21ſt of June, 1791, the flight to Varennes.

———— 21ſt of Sept. 1792, the abolition of royalty.

———— 21ſt of Jan. 1793, his decapitation.*

——but let me quit this diſagreeable ſubject.

There is nothing beyond the power of accident. If it be a million to one that an event ſhall not happen, it is ſtill one to a million that it may happen, and therefore

* It is an odd circumſtance, that one of the King of France's Council ſhould be named *Target*; which is the dramatic name of a Counſellor in The *Conſcious Lovers*. Nothing can be more ſerious and affecting than the trial of Louis XVI. but this unfortunate name, *Target*, to an Engliſhman, occaſions an aſſociation of ideas totally abhorrent to the ſenſations which would elſe be excited by ſuch ſevere diſtreſs.

fore within poffibility.—I will mention a coincidence which had more chances againft it than any I have yet mentioned. I once faw five keys, belonging to a ftranger, connected with a ring, which were fo precifely the counterpart of other five keys and a ring in my poffeffion, that there was no diftinguifhing between them in any refpect—the keys were of very different ages and fizes, and the rings particularly formed—I leave it to mathematicians to calculate the odds againft this coincidence, which is all but miraculous.

On

On *Literary Thievery*.

INSTANCES have been given of Sterne's borrowing, perhaps, ſtealing, ſome thoughts and paſſages from Burton's Anatomy of Melancholy. As I myſelf never ſteal, at leaſt, knowingly, it may be expected that I ſhould cry out vehe-mently againſt thieves. Whether my principles and practice are, as uſual, at variance, or whether that rogue Falſtaff has given me medicines to make me love the *vocation* becauſe it was his, I know not; but I am willing to let all ſuch thieves as Sterne eſcape puniſhment—I ſay this to avoid the ſuſpicion of malice, in bringing two or three additional in-ſtances of the uſe Sterne has made of his reading.

The

The Note C. in the article Francis d'Affifi of Bayle's Dictionary, contains the doctrine which Sterne has fo whimfically applied in his Triftram Shandy— " I wifh my father, fays he, had minded " what he was about, &c."*—Bayle fays, " one of the moft celebrated of Ariftotle's " Commentators maintained, that the " public welfare requires, that, in this " action, &c."*—Again, Gafpar a Rees fays, " that wife and thoughtful men, " &c."*

Bayle has alfo furnifhed Sterne with the names of Rebours and La Fofieufe, and many little circumftances in his ftory of *The Whifkers*, which may be found in the article of Margaret de Valois, together

---

* If the reader turns to thefe paffages he will fee that they could not decently be quoted ; which is a great difadvantage to my pofition, as the imitation is fo manifeft.

R 3

ther with the name of La Fleur a foot-
man, and a little trait of his character.*

In Montaigne is a Chapter on Names,
which Sterne has imitated, and much improved. The following paſſage from
that author probably gave Sterne the firſt
hint of Obadiah's Adventure with Dr.
Slop at the turning of the garden wall.
" In the time of our third, or ſecond
" troubles (I do not remember which)
" going one day abroad to take the air,
" about a league from my own houſe,
" which is ſeated in the very centre of
" all the buſtle and miſchief of the late
" civil wars of France—thinking myſelf
" in all ſecurity, and ſo near to my re-
" treat that I ſtood in need of no better
" equipage; I had taken a horſe that
                                    " went

* It is to be found in the New Voyage into
Terra Auſtralis, by James Sadeur (a feigned name).
This book ſeems alſo to be the original of ſome
paſſages in De Foe, and of Addiſon's Allegory of
the Androgynes, though he refers to Plato.

" went very eafy upon his pace, but was
" not very ftrong. Being upon my re-
" turn home (a fudden occafion falling
" out to make ufe of this horfe in a kind
" of fervice that he was not acquainted
" with) one of my train, a lufty fellow,
" mounted upon a ftrong German horfe,
" that had a very ill mouth, but was
" otherwife vigorous and unfoiled, to
" play the bravo, and appear a better
" man than his fellows, comes thunder-
" ing full-fpeed in the very track where
" I was, rufhing, like a Coloffus, upon
" the little man, and the little horfe,
" with fuch a career of ftrength and
" weight, that he turned us both over
" and over topfy-turvy, with our heels
" in the air—fo that there lay the horfe
" overthrown and ftunned with the fall,
" and I ten paces from him, ftretched
" out at length, with my face all bat-
" tered and broken, my fword which I
" had in my hand, above ten paces be-
" yond that, my belt broke all to pieces,

R 4   " &c."

" &c." In adventures of this fort there is always a little dash of the ridiculous mixed with the misfortune. It is worth remarking, how Sterne has abated of the misfortune, and added to the ridicule.

Trim's Differtation on Death, and Remarks on the fame fubject from Mr. Shandy and Uncle Toby, feem to originate from thefe reflections of Montaigne —" I have often confidered with myfelf,
" whence it fhould proceed, that war,
" the image of death, whether we look
" upon it as to our own particular dan-
" ger, or that of another, fhould, with-
" out comparifon, appear lefs dreadful
" than at home in our own houfes, and
" that being ftill in all places the fame,
" there fhould be, notwithftanding, more
" affurance in peafants, and the meaner
" fort of people, than others of better
" quality and education; and I do verily
" believe, that it is thofe terrible cere-
" monies and preparations, wherewith
                                        " we

" we fet it out, that more terrify us than
" the thing itfelf."*

As I have already declared myfelf in
perfect charity with " a clean neat-
handed thief;" for the above inftances I
have only inftituted a court of enquiry—
but if Sterne fhould be indicted for the
next thievery, he has no other way of
getting off, but by pleading " his clergy."

In the year 1697, were publifhed,
Twelve Sermons by Walter Leightenhoufe, Prebendary of Lincoln. From
the Twelfth of thefe Sermons I have extracted the following paffages, which will
be found in the Seventh pofthumous
Sermon of Sterne, word for word, except
where the difference is noted.

" The

---

* If my reader loves Montaigne half as well as
I do, he will pardon the length of thefe quotations,
which are taken from Cotton's Tranflation.

[250]

*(Sterne)
" It is obfer-
vable that the
ApoftlePaul"

‡ "And on
that ground
builds a rock
of encourage-
ment for fu-
ture, &c."
This is alter-
ed for the
worfe—we
may build a
fortrefs, but
not a rock—
however, this
very expref-
fion is taken
from Leigh-
tenhoufe, p.
434, "builds
a rock of en-
couragement
not only for
himfelf, &c."

" The Apoſtle St. Paul* en-
" couraging the Corinthians to
" bear with patience the tryals
" incident to human nature,
" reminds them of the delive-
" rance that God did formerly
" vouchfafe to him, and his
" fellow-labourers, Gaius and
" Ariſtarcus, and thence builds
" a fortreſs‡ of future truſt and
" dependance on him; his life
" had been in very great jeo-
" pardy at Epheſus, where he
" had like to have been brought
" out to the Theatre to have
" been devoured by wild beaſts;
" and indeed had no human
" means to avert and confe-
" quently to efcape it. And
" therefore he tells them, that
" he had this advantage by it,
" that the more he believed he
" fhould be put to death; the
" more he was engaged by his
" deliverance

" deliverance never to depend on any
" worldly truft, but only on God, who
" can refcue from the greateft extremity,
" even from the grave or death itfelf.
" For we would not, Brethren, fays he,
" have you ignorant of our trouble which
" came to us in Afia, that we were
" preffed out of meafure, above ftrength,
" infomuch that we defpaired of life.
" But as we had the fentence of death in
" ourfelves, that we fhould not truft in
" ourfelves, but in God, which raifeth
" the dead: who delivered us from fo
" great a death, and doth deliver: in
" whom we truft, that he will deliver
" us. And indeed a ftronger argument
" cannot be brought for future affiance
" than paft deliverance; for what ground
" or reafon can I have to diftruft the
" kindnefs of that perfon who hath al-
" ways been my friend and benefactor?
" On whom can I better rely for affif-
" tance in the day of my diftrefs, than
" on him who ftood by me in all mine
" affliction;

" affliction; and when I was at the very
" brink of deſtruction delivered me out
" of all my troubles? Would it not be
" highly ungrateful, and reflect either
" upon his goodneſs or ſufficiency, to
" diſtruſt that providence which hath al-
" ways had a watchful eye over me; and
" who, according to his gracious pro-
" miſes, would never yet leave me, nor
" forſake me?

Again—
" Haſt thou ever laid upon the bed
" of languiſhing, or laboured under any
" grievous diſtemper? Call to mind thy
" ſorrowful penſive ſpirit at that time,
" and add to it who it was that had
" mercy on thee, and brought thee out
" of darkneſs and the ſhadow of death,
" and made all thy bed in ſickneſs. Hath
" the ſcantineſs of thy condition hurried
" thee into great ſtraights and difficul-
" ties, and brought thee almoſt to thy
" wit's end? Conſider who it was that
                                " ſpread

" fpread thy table in that wildernefs of
" thoughts, and made thy cup to over-
" flow, &c. &c."

Thefe are pretty ftrong inftances of
the liberties that one preacher takes with
another, and it ought to make publifhers
of pofthumous fermons a little careful,
left, inftead of their friend's compofition,
they may only republifh what has already
been printed—perhaps more than once
before. Leightenhoufe has not only furnifhed Sterne with matter, but feems alfo
to have been his original for that dramatic
caft in his Sermons, fo engaging to fome,
and fo difagreeable to others.

I now part with Sterne—but it is to
put him in better company.

" A criminal about to be executed,
" anfwered his confeffor, who promifed
" him he fhould that day fup with the
" Lord—Do you go then, faid he, in
                                    " my

" my room, for I keep faft to day."
(Montaigne.) This repartee gave Prior
the fubject for his ballad of the *Thief and
Cordelier*—but he has much improved
the wit, by making the prieft allege his
fafting, in compliance with the rules of
the church, prevented him from fupping
in Paradife in the room of the criminal.
The fong is too well known to need
quotation.

Affuredly we owe the exiftence of
Prior's Alma, one of the moft finifhed
and original Poems in our language, to
the following paffage from Montaigne.
" The natural heat firft feats itfelf in the
" feet—that concerns infancy. Then it
" mounts into the middle region, where
" it makes a long abode, and produces,
" in my opinion, the only true pleafure
" of human life ; all other pleafures,- in
" comparifon, fleep. Towards the end;
" like a vapour that ftill mounts upward;
" it arrives at the throat, where it makes
" its

" its final refidence, and concludes the
" progrefs." If this had been written
after the Poem, it would have paffed for
an abridgement of it—perhaps, Prior's
calling it the *Progrefs* of the mind, might·
have been occafioned by the laft word
of the quotation. Befides taking Montaigne's ideas as the plan of his Poem, he
has verfified the above paffage as a pro-
fpectus of the whole defign.

> My fimple fyftem fhall fuppofe,
> That Alma enters at the toes;
> That then fhe mounts by juft degrees,
> Up to the ancles, legs, and knees;
> Next, as the fap of life does rife,
> She lends her vigor to the thighs:
> And, all thefe under-regions paft,
> She neftles fomewhere near the wafte:
> Gives pain or pleafure, grief or laughter;
> As we fhall fhow at large hereafter.
> Mature, if not improv'd, by time,
> Up to the heart fhe loves to climb:
> From thence, compell'd by craft and age,
> She makes the head her lateft ftage.

It has been often faid, that Voltaire is
much obliged to Englifh literature—he
is

is fo, but then it is in fuch a fort as to
do honour to the fources of his imitation.

Who but himfelf could have made
the following paffages fo dexteroufly his
own?

> " There is a tall long-fided dame
> (But wondrous light) ycleped Fame
> *   *   *   *
>
> Two trumpets fhe does found at once,
> But both of clean contrary tones;
> But whether both with the fame wind,
> Or one before and one behind,
> &c. &c."
>
> HUDIBRAS.

> " La Renommèe a toujours deux Trompettes,
> L'une à fa bouche appliquèe à propos,
> Va celebrant les Exploits des Heros,
> L'autre eft au cu" — — —
>
> LA PUCELLE.

> As an owl that's in the barn
> Sees a moufe creeping in the corn,
> Sits ftill, and fhuts his round blue eyes
> As if he flept, until he fpies
> The little beaft within his reach,
> Then ftarts, and feizes on the wretch.
>
> HUDIBRAS.

Ainfi

" Ainſi qu'un chat qui, d'un regard avide
Guette au paſſage une ſouris timide,
Marchant tout doux, la terre ne ſent pas
L'Impreſſion de ces pieds delicats,
Dés qu'il l'a vue, il a ſautè ſur elle."

LA PUCELLE.

The thievery of a fool is never ex-
cuſed, becauſe no one can return the
compliment; but, we pardon a genius,
becauſe if he takes, he is qualified to give
in return. The great natural poſſeſſions
of Sterne, Prior, and Voltaire, will afford ample reſources to thoſe of their
ſucceſſors who have abilities to make re-
priſals.

S   *On*

On Pope's Epitaphs.

" If there is any writer whose genius can embellish
impropriety, and whose authority can make error
venerable, his works are the proper objects of critical inquisition."

RAMBLER, No. 139.

AN endeavour to restore fame where
it has been taken away, is a pleasing employment; but if it be necessarily connected with the same fault in yourself
which you wish to correct in another,
there seems cause for at least as much
pain as pleasure.

I am in this very predicament—and
hope my intention to reinstate a poet in
his ancient honours, will be held as an
equivalent to any just motive which may
be assigned for abating the credit of his
critic—I wish the one could be done with-

out

out the other—and muſt beg to have it remembered, that this is not an attack upon Johnſon, but a vindication of Pope.

The deſire of having a dead friend re-membered by a good Epitaph, occaſions frequent applications to thoſe poets who enjoy public reputation, which they are expected to comply with, as if anſwering a demand for a commodity in which they dealt. Pope, I believe, had nothing of this ſort to diſpoſe of, unleſs his heart very powerfully ſeconded the application —in conſequence, his Epitaphs have ge-nerally a pathetic caſt, and ſeem rather intended to affect our feelings, than to be objects of criticiſm. Dr. Johnſon thought differently—my intention is to hyper-criticize his criticiſm. Where I could abridge his remarks without prejudice to the ſenſe, I have done it. The Epitaphs for the moſt part could not be abridged; which forces me to tranſcribe (what I would willingly have avoided) lines ſo

well-

well known, and once so much ap-
plauded.

On *the* EARL *of* DORSET.

* (1) Dorset, the grace of courts, the Muses pride,
(2) Patron of arts, and judge of nature, dy'd.
The scourge of pride, though sanctify'd or great,
Of fops in learning, and of knaves in state. (3)
Yet soft in nature, (4) though severe his lay,
His anger moral, and his wisdom gay.
(5) Blest satyrist! who touch'd the mean so true
As shew'd, vice had his hate and pity too.
Blest courtier! who could King and country please,
Yet (6) sacred kept his friendship and his ease.
Blest peer! his great forefather's every grace
Reflecting, and reflected on his race ;
Where other Buckhursts, other Dorsets shine
And patriots still, or poets, deck the line!

POPE.

(*Johnson.*) " The first distich of this
Epitaph contains a kind of information
which few would want—that the man
for

---

* The same references do for the Epitaph, Criticism, and Reply, which, in reading, should *follow*
each other. In some instances, the Criticism and
Reply are necessarily without a corresponding number in the Epitaph.

for whom the tomb was erected (1) died, &c. What is meant by *judge of nature,* is not eafy to fay. Nature is not the object of human judgment; for it is vain to judge where we cannot alter. If by nature is meant what is commonly called *nature* by the critics, a juft reprefentation of things really exifting and actions really performed, nature cannot be properly oppofed to art; nature being in this fenfe only the beft effect of art." (2)

" The fcourge of pride"—

POPE.

" Of this couplet, the fecond line is not, what is intended, an illuftration of the former, pride in the great, is indeed well enough connected with knaves in ftate * * * but the mention of *fanctified* pride will not lead the thoughts to *fops in learning* * * * but to fomething more gloomy and more formidable than foppery." (3)

S 3

" Yet

" Yet foft his nature"

POPE.

" This is a high compliment, but was not firft beftowed on Dorfet by Pope. (4) The next verfe is extremely beautiful;

" Bleft fatyrift"—

POPE.

" In this diftich is another line, of which Pope was not the author. (5) * * *

" Bleft courtier"—

POPE.

" Whether a courtier can be properly commended for keeping his *eafe facred*, may, perhaps, be difputable. * * * I wifh our poets would attend a little more accurately to the ufe of the word (6) *facred*, which furely fhould never be applied in a ferious compofition, but where fome reference may be made to a higher Being, or where fome duty is exacted or implied. * * * I know not whether this Epitaph be

be worthy either of the writer or of the
man entombed." (7)

(*Reply.*) (1) The poet's meaning is
very clear, unlefs it be purpofely per-
verted—" Neither the rank nor accomplifhments of Dorfet exempted him from
the common lot of all men"—this was
not intended for information, but it is a
natural reflection. (2) " A patron to
artifts, and himfelf a philofopher."

(3) " He was the fcourge of pride
wherefoever he found it—he corrected
thofe pretenfions to learning where va-
nity was predominant, and had no refpect
to knaves in power." (4) If this was
his real character, fhould it be fuppreffed
becaufe it had been faid before? Befides,
it has nothing particular, and may be
juftly faid of many, without incurring the
cenfure of plagiarifm.

(5) This

(5) This is an affertion without proof —as it is in the nature of an accufation, it ought to have been fupported.

(6) The word " *facred*" is frequently ufed without the leaft idea of a religious application—

> " *Sacred* to ridicule his whole life long,
> And the fad burthen of fome merry fong."
>
> POPE.

Nay, it required not Dr. Johnfon's learning to know, that the Latin word from whence it is derived, fometimes fignifies the very reverfe to any thing fet apart for *divine* ufes—

> Ego fum malus, ego fum *facer*, fceleftus.
>
> PLAUTUS.

(7) It is worthy of both for ought that has appeared to the contrary—however, there is a fault, which, as it efcaped the notice of the poet (who furely had the beft ear of the two) his critic

may

may be excufed for not difcovering.—
This is the jingle of the fame found, occafioned by the blameable repetition of
" *pride*" in the firft and third lines.

On Sir W. Trumbal.

A pleafing form, a firm, yet cautious mind,
Sincere, though prudent; conftant, yet refign'd;
Honour unchang'd, a principle profeft,
Fix'd to one fide, but moderate to the reft;
An honeft courtier, (9) yet a patriot too, (10)
Juft to his prince, and to his country true.
(11) Fill'd with the fenfe of age, the fire of youth,
A fcorn of wrangling, yet a zeal for truth;
A generous faith, from fuperftition free;
A love to peace, and hate of tyranny;
Such this man was; who now, from earth remov'd
(12) At length enjoys that liberty he lov'd.

Pope.

(*Johnfon.*) " In this Epitaph * * is a
fault * * the name is omitted (8) * * *
There is an oppofition between an *honeft
courtier* and a *patriot*; for an honeft
courtier cannot but be a *patriot* (9) * *
It was unfuitable to the nicety required
in fhort compofitions, to clofe his verfe
with

with the word *too* (10) * * *Fill'd* is
weak and profaic (11) * * * The thought
in the laft line is impertinent * * * it
would have been juft and pathetic if applied to Bernardi, who died in prifon
after a confinement of forty years without
a crime; but why fhould Trumbal be
congratulated on his liberty, who had
never known reftraint? (12)

(*Reply.*) (8) Undoubtedly, a fault in
the Epitaph.

(9) Moft certainly, an " *honeft*" man
is fo in all ftations, but Pope himfelf ex-
plains his meaning " He was juft to his
prince (an honeft courtier) and true to
his country (a patriot too)."

(10) To be fure, if this monofyllable
be taken out of its place, and looked at
very particularly, there is nothing in it.
to engage much attention—for this the
poet is not accountable.

(11) The

(11) The foregoing remark will in part apply to this—in fact, there is nothing of sufficient confequence to juftify any obfervation.

(12) Dr. Johnfon's religion undoubtedly taught him, that the foul, when united to the body, is in a ftate of confinement—" When fhall I be delivered from this body of death?" exclaims St. Paul—" While we are confined in this *penfold* here," fays Milton. There is nothing new or particular in this : the doctrine is held by all orthodox believers, in which number theDoctor is moft furelyincluded.

On the Honorable S. HARCOURT.

To this fad fhrine, whoe'er thou art, draw near,
Here lies the friend moft lov'd, the fon moft dear,
Who ne'er knew joy, but friendfhip might divide,
Or gave his father grief, but when he died.

How vain is reafon, eloquence how weak !
If Pope muft tell what Harcourt cannot fpeak.
Oh ! let thy once-lov'd friend infcribe thy ftone,
And with a father's forrow mix his own.

POPE.

(*Johnson.*) " The *name* in this Epitaph is inferted with a peculiar felicity, &c. * * * I wifh the two laft lines had been omitted, as they take away from the energy what they do not add to the fenfe." (13)

(*Reply,*) (13) There is a better reafon ftill—the firft quatrain ends with " Or gave his *father* grief, but when he died"— the fecond ends with " And with a *father's* forrow mix his own"—The word *father* in fo fhort a piece fhould not have been repeated at all, but if there had been a neceffity for it, the repetition fhould not have been in the fame part of the line.

On JAMES CRAGGS, *Efq.*

JACOBUS CRAGGS
Regi magnæ Britanniæ, &c. &c.

* * * * *

Statefman, yet friend to truth! of foul fincere,
In action faithful, and in honour clear, (14)
Who broke no promife, ferv'd no private end,
Who gain'd no title, and who loft no friend, (15)
Eanobled by, himfelf, by all approv'd;
Prais'd, wept, and honour'd by the Mufe he lov'd.

POPE.

(*Johnſon.*) * * * " There is a redundancy of words in the firſt couplet : it is ſuperfluous to tell of him who was *ſincere, true,* and *faithful,* that he was in honour *clear.* (14) There ſeems to be an oppoſition intended in the fourth line, which is not very obvious : where is the wonder that he who *gain'd no title,* ſhould *loſe no friend?* (15) * * * It is abſurd to join in the ſame inſcription Latin and Engliſh, or verſe and proſe," (16) &c.

(*Reply.*) (14) It is true that the epithets of *themſelves* are of the ſame claſs, but if connected with their ſubſtantives, the ſameneſs ceaſes. Beſides, the oppoſition between " Stateſman, yet friend to truth" takes " true" out of the catalogue. Surely, though a ſincere ſoul includes all virtues, yet, in detail it is different from being " faithful in action," or " clear in honour."

(15) There

(15) There is certainly no opposition between " title" and " friend," but there is between " gain'd" and " lost," which are sufficient for all the *effect* of opposition.

(16) It is undoubtedly, false taste.

On *Mr.* ROWE.

Thy reliques, Rowe, &c. &c.
*   *   *   *
Peace to thy gentle shade, (17) &c.

POPE.

(*Johnson.*) * * * " To wish, *peace to thy shade* (17) is too mythological to be admitted into a Christian Temple, the ancient worship has infected almost all our other compositions, and might therefore be contented to spare our Epitaphs. " Let fiction cease with life, &c. &c."

(*Reply.*) (17) As Dr. Johnson (like Parson Adams) " though he was not afraid of ghosts, did not absolutely disbelieve

lieve

lieve them," why fhould he object to the word " fhade?" Would " foul" have been better? But, as Trim fays, that would have been but a " Popifh fhift."

On *Mrs.* Corbet.
(Nothing particular.)

On the *Honourable* Robert Digby.
(Nothing remarked, except)

(*Johnfon.*) " The fcantinefs of human praifes can fcarcely be made more apparent, than by remarking how often Pope has, in the few Epitaphs which he compofed, found it neceffary to borrow from himfelf. (18)

(*Reply.*) (18) It ought to be remembered, that each Epitaph is a fingle unconnected thing, and has nothing to do with any other—that it is the critic, and not the poet, that has brought them to quarrel with each other, or to agree
where

where they ought to differ. It is certain, that all thefe Epitaphs together make but an exceeding fmall body of poetry, but it is as certain, that no other poet has made fo many that were really infcribed upon monuments.

On *Sir* GODFREY KNELLER.

Kneller, &c. ● ● ●
Lies crown'd (19) with prince's honours, poet's lays.

POPE.

(*Johnfon*.) The third couplet is deformed by a broken metaphor, the word "*crowned*" (19) not being applicable to the "*honours*" or the "*lays.*"

(*Reply.*) (19) To crown with *honour*, or *glory*, is juftified by common ufe.

" Crown me with glory, take who will the bays"
And
" With honour let defert be crown'd."

Certainly neither Honour nor Glory are tangible fubftances, and of courfe cannot
be

be put upon the head—it is needlefs to
dwell on fuch objections.

On General WITHERS.

*   *   *   *

(20) O! born to arms! O worth in youth approv'd;
O foft humanity in age belov'd!
For thee the hardy veteran drops a tear,
And the gay courtier feels the figh fincere. (21)

*   *   *   *

POPE.

(*Johnfon.*)   * * *   " The particle O!
(20) ufed at the beginning of a fentence,
always offends * *   There is fomething
of the common cant of fuperficial faty-
rifts, to fuppofe, that the infincerity (21)
of a courtier deftroys all his fenfations,
&c.   At the third couplet I fhould wifh
the Epitaph to clofe, (22) &c. &c.

(*Reply.*)   (20) The double repetition
of " O" certainly offends.   (21) I believe it is a generally received opinion,
that diffimulation is a neceffary part of a
courtier's character, which is fufficient to
juftify the expreffion.

T   (22) If

(22) If the Epitaph had ended here, it would have had nothing to mark the conclusion.

On Mr. E. FENTON.

This modeſt ſtone, what few vain marbles can,
May truly ſay, here lies an honeſt man, (23)
A poet, bleſt beyond the poet's fate,
Whom Heaven kept ſacred from the proud and great:
Foe to loud praiſe, and friend to learned eaſe,
Content with ſcience in the vale of peace.
Calmly he look'd on either life; and here
Saw nothing to regret, or there to fear;
From nature's temperate feaſt roſe ſatisfy'd,
Thank'd Heav'n that he had liv'd and that he dy'd.

POPE.

(*Johnſon.*) " The firſt couplet of this Epitaph is borrowed. (23) The four next lines contain a ſpecies of praiſe peculiar, original, and juſt. (24) Here, therefore, the inſcription ſhould have ended, the latter part containing nothing but what is common to every man who is wiſe and good, (25) &c."

(*Reply.*)

(*Reply.*) (23) It is common enough to fay, " Here lies an honeft man"—the Epitaph takes off from the objection, by hinting, that upon few tombftones it has a right to be engraved.

(24) See (22):

(25) To be in general " wife and good" was the real character of Fenton —there were no particular traits in it.

On Mr. GAY:

Of manners (26) gentle, of affections mild ;
In wit, a man ; fimplicity, a child :
With native humour tempering virtuous rage, (28)
Form'd to delight at once, and lafh the age : (29)
Above temptation, in a low eftate,
And uncorrupted, ev'n among the great :
A fafe companion (30) and an eafy friend,
Unblam'd thro' life, lamented in thy end, (31)
Thefe are thy honours ! not that here thy buft
Is mix'd with heroes, or with kings thy duft ;
But that the worthy and the good fhall fay,
Striking their penfive bofoms—Here lies Gay.

POPE.

T 2   (*Johnfon.*)

(*Johnson.*) * * * " The two parts of the firſt line are only echoes of each other; "*gentle manners*" and "*mild* (26) *affections,*" if they mean anything, muſt mean the ſame.

" That Gay was a "*man in wit*" is a very frigid commendation; to have the *wit of a man* is not much for a poet. " The wit (27) of *man,*" and the "*ſim-plicity of a child,*" make a poor and vulgar contraſt, and raiſe no ideas of excellence, either intellectual or moral.

" In the next couplet "*rage*" is leſs properly introduced after the mention of "*mildneſs*" and "*gentleneſs,*" which are made the conſtituents of his character; for a man ſo "*mild*" and "*gentle*" to "*tem-per*" his "*rage*" was not difficult. (28)

" The next line is unharmonious in its ſound, and mean in its conception; the oppoſition is obvious, and the word "*laſh*"

" *lafh*" ufed abfolutely, and without any modification, is grofs and improper. (29)

* * * to be a " *fafe* (30) *companion*" is praife merely negative, arifing not from the poffeffion of virtue, but the abfence of vice, and that one of the moft odious.

" As little can be added to his character, by afferting that he was " *lamented in his end.*" Every man that dies, is, at leaft by (31) the writer of his Epitaph, fuppofed to be lamented, and therefore this general lamentation does no honour to Gay.

" The eight firft lines have no grammar; (32) the adjectives are without any fubftantive, and the epithets without a fubject.

" The thought in the laft line, that Gay is buried in the bofoms of the " *worthy*" and the " *good,*" who are diftin-

guifhed

guiſhed only to lengthen the line, is ſo
dark, that few underſtand it; and ſo
harſh, when it is explained, that ſtill
fewer approve. (33)

(*Reply.*) (26) It is true, that "*gentle*"
and "*mild*" are of the ſame family, but
I never knew before that "manners" and
"affeſtions" were the ſame—our manners may be mild, and our affeſtions
ſtrong, or our manners may be rough,
and our affeſtions weak, or they may
both be violent, or mild; which latter
was Gay's charaſter.

(27) He was in wiſdom (for ſo *wit* *
means in this place) a mature man, but
as artleſs as a child—I believe this was
never but *once* conſidered as a poor and
vulgar contraſt, nor could I have thought
it

---

* This was its firſt ſignification—"*mother-wit*"
—" I thought you had more *wit*, &c. &c.".

it *ever* had failed in raising ideas of excellence, both intellectual and moral.

(28) As he was a virtuous man he was displeased (a poet may say, *enraged*) at the vices of the times, but as he was a man of humour, he might express his indignation rather like Horace than Juvenal—this is the natural meaning of the passage.

(29) See (28) for the poet's thought —the objection to *lash* I do not understand.

(30) If to be a " *safe companion* and an *easy friend*" be only *negative* praise, let no one pretend to praise *positive*. If there are two virtues more particularly pleasing in society than any other, they are those which Pope found in his friend, and published to the world in his Epitaph. —As the whole is universally read with emotions of sympathy and tenderness,

T 4   this

this line in particular juſtifies the propriety of our ſenſations.

(31) To uſe an expreſſion of Dr.
Johnſon's own, " there is a *frigidity*" in
this, which ſets at nought all attempts
to enliven it.

'(32) If they have not grammar they
have taſte and feeling, which were ſubjects not ſo well underſtood by the critic
—but why have they not grammar? Is
it ſo unuſual to delay, in conſtruction,
the *firſt* part of a ſentence until the end
of it?·

> " Of man's firſt diſobedience, &c.
> * * * ſing heav'nly muſe."

Is it neceſſary to explain this? " Sing hea-
venly muſe of man's firſt diſobedience,
&c."—In like manner, " Theſe are thy
honours, to be of manners gentle, &c."—
It ſhould be obſerved, that though " *to*
be"

be" was neceffary in my explanation, it is not fo for the original.

(33) It is confeffed that there is but a fhade of difference between " worthy and good;" but if there were none, fuch pleonafms are common enough; particularly in the Common Prayer, " we have *erred* and *ftrayed* from thy ways"—" we are *tyed* and *bound*, &c." The expreffion *here lies*, as commonly ufed, admitting but of one fenfe, and that fixed by long cuftom; it cannot (though for a better) be eafily departed from.

Intended for Sir I. NEWTON.

ISAACUS NEWTONIUS
Quem immortalem
Teftantur, Tempus, Natura, Cœlum:
Mortalem (34)
Hoc Marmor fatetur.

Nature, and nature's laws, lay hid in night:
God faid, *Let Newton be!* and all was light.

POPE.

(*Johnfon.*)

(*Johnson.*) " Of this Epitaph, short as it is, the faults seem not to be very few. * * * In the Latin, the opposition of *immortalis* and *mortalis*, is a mere sound or a mere quibble; he is not immortal in any sense contrary to that in which he is mortal. (34)

" In the verses the thought is obvious, and the words " *night*" and " *light*" are too nearly allied." (35)

(*Reply.*) (34) He is immortal (that is, as long as science exists) by his great discoveries in natural philosophy; but by his tomb we find him to be mortal—no one before ever found any difficulty or impropriety.

. It is obvious from whence Pope took the allusion, and it ought to be so; but that is different from the *thought* being obvious. (35) " *Night*" and " *light*" to the ear are more alike than to the eye.

On Edmund *Duke of* Buckingham.

Who died in the Nineteenth Year of his Age.

If modeſt youth with cool reflection crown'd, (36)
And every opening (37) virtue blooming round,

(38) ⎰ Could ſave a parent's juſteſt pride from fate,
⎪ Or add one patriot to a ſinking ſtate ;
⎪ This weeping marble had not aſk'd thy tear,
⎨ Or ſadly told, how many hopes lie here !
⎪ The living virtue now had ſhone approv'd,
⎱ The Senate heard him, and his country lov'd.

Yet ſofter honours, and leſs noiſy fame,
Attend the ſhade of gentle Buckingham :
In whom a race, for courage fam'd and art, (39)
Ends in the milder merit of the heart ;
And chiefs or ſages long to Britain given
Pay the laſt tribute of a Saint to Heaven.

Pope.

(*Johnſon*.) * * * " To " *crown*"
with " reflection" is ſurely a mode of
ſpeech approaching to nonſenſe. " *Opening virtues blooming round*" is ſomething
like tautology ; the ſix following lines are
poor and proſaic. (38) " *Art*" is uſed
for " *arts*," that a rhyme may be had to
" *heart*," &c."

(*Reply.*)

(*Reply.*) (36) To crown with reflection is certainly not very correct—this expreſſion cannot be juſtified by (19)—yet, we ſay, the end *crowns* all—as the crowning of a king is the greateſt honour he can receive, ſo a fortunate ending puts the crown on former actions.

(37) If we *muſt* take exception to this phraſe, we ſhould rather think it a contradiction than a tautology—flowers that are *opening* cannot be ſaid to be *blooming* —but the firſt poet in the univerſe may be diſſected in this manner, until he loſes both ſubſtance and form, and is reduced to nothing !

(38) What is generally underſtood by proſaic, is, ſentences having the common form of ſtructure—whereas poetry conſiſts of inverſions, and a dignity of expreſſion, which ſuit not with proſe. If theſe lines be examined upon this principle,

ciple, the objection will be found to have
no force.

(39) " *Art*" for " *arts*" is not to be
defended.

There is an expreffion in this Epitaph,
which, though not uncommon, is improper. " This weeping marble," no
doubt, every one underftands without
explanation—but it is impoffible not to
attend to the *immediate* meaning—marble, on which moifture is condenfed in
drops—and which, in fact, is much more
like tears, than a Cupid with his hand to
his eyes. I fee all the poverty and mean-
nefs of fuch a conceit, but it really ob-
trudes itfelf on the imagination, in confequence of " marble" being mentioned
inftead of the fculptured figure.

The Hermit.

Not long fince a Gentleman, whofe real name I fhall difguife under that of Adraftus, took it into his head to give up, or rather to fhun fociety, and retire to a poor cottage, which may ftill be found between Brecknock and the neighbouring mountain called the Beacon. The place, tho' lonely, was not fecluded from obfervation—befides, he was obliged to attend the market at Brecknock for neceffaries, fo that it was well known fuch a perfon was there, and lived by himfelf. It is true, that once a day a middle-aged woman called at the houfe to clean it, which when fhe had done, fhe departed; and now and then a perfon going by would afk if he wanted any thing from the town—with thefe excep-

tions,

tions, he might be faid to live abfolutely alone. Acquaintance he had none, altho' he cheerfully joined in fuch converfation as chance threw in his way. If the weather was unfavourable, he ftaid at home— when it was fine, he explored the vales, or afcended the mountains of the beautiful country he had chofen for his refidence. As his pace was fometimes flow and folemn, and at other times quick and impetuous, his air was not like one of this world, efpecially as he would at times paufe to look at fome trifling object, and feem to obferve a great deal where the common eye could fee nothing. Thefe, and other circumftances, occafioned Adraftus to be confidered as a peculiar character, and, tho' always mentioned as a whimfical being, yet, as no one found he did any harm, he was left to purfue his vagaries in peace. Almoft the greateft favor the world has to beftow !

One

One fummer-morning, carrying his day's provifion in his pocket, he afcended the Beacon, and feated himfelf on the edge of that rapid defcent which over-looks the vale of the Ufke. He was alone, it is true, but the furrounding ob-jects furnifhed fuch a quick fucceffion of ideas, that before he could half finifh one fubject, another prefented itfelf for con-fideration, and altogether produced that agreeable tumult of the mind which is fuppofed to be found only in fociety. The keen air of the place reminding him of his dinner, he drew forth his cold mutton and bread, unconfcious of being obferved, and was eating with a fenfation of pleafure unknown where it is endea-voured to be excited at a great expence.

" Suppofe you wafhed it down with a glafs of punch," faid a gentleman behind him, who made one of a large party of both fexes, that had come from Brecon to fpend a day on the mountain—" Very willingly,

willingly, Sir," replied Adraſtus, who was too collected and firm in himſelf to be alarmed at an unexpected addreſs. He aroſe from the turf, and joined the company, who were mixing their ſhrub from the adjoining natural baſin of pureſt water.

" Pray Sir," ſays the ſtranger, " can you poſſibly account for this ſpring on the top of a mountain ? or for that round baſin that is down in yonder hollow, which they tell me is unfathomable ?" " Perhaps," replied Adraſtus, " I might give a ſatisfactory anſwer to your queſtion, but it would be encroaching too much upon the ſubjects of general converſation." " It was the very ſubject which engaged our attention," replied the other, " and the ſhorteſt way of introducing a new one would be to diſpatch this." " The ſpring," ſaid Adraſtus, " may poſſibly be ſupplied by the vapours which moſt commonly reſt on the mountain head, or it

U   may

may afcend from below like water through fand—perhaps both caufes are combined —the circumftance is common, and we need not recur to any extraordinary prin- ciple."

The ladies were liftening to the moun- tain-philofopher with great attention; when the guide whifpered who it was they had accidentally met, and gave all the traits of his character the fhort time afforded. The converfation now had more of the company to join in it—" The water is delicious," fays a lady, " and makes admirable punch," faid a gentle- man—" But, there is the punch-*bowl* be- low," faid another, pointing down to the lake—" That bowl," pleafantly replied Adraftus, " was once as full of fire as it is now of water"—here he was inter- rupted by a general interjection of fur- prize—he continued—" This mountain was once a volcano; that round bafin is the crater—it bears a general refemblance

to

to twenty other mountains in Wales, all which have their craters; now become fmall circular lakes of a vaft depth."

This language was by no means underftood by the company, who knew more of punch-bowls than craters, and poor Adraftus was confidered as a little cracked, by all, but the perfon to whom the guide had defcribed him, who very oddly conceived an idea, which afterwards produced a refolution we fhall again have an occafion to mention.

When the ham, cold beef, and chicken-pye were eaten, and the punch drank; the company having finifhed their bufinefs, bade adieu to Adraftus, and departed. He traced them down the different ftages of the mountain, remarking the diminution of objects by diftance, and their increafing faintnefs by aerial perfpective. After waiting to fee the full-moon in oppofition to the fetting fun, he

alfo

alfo defcended; and with his ufual occupation of mind came home—but the
moon furveyed through his telefcope
robbed him of fome hours repofe.

As the company proceeded to Brecon,
the guide acquainted them more at large
with all he knew, and all he had heard of
Adraftus: and although a great part of
the latter was untrue, yet that perfon
mentioned above, and whom we will call
Crito, who was one of thofe characters
that fancy themfelves geniufes—that they
have tafte, and prefume to be critics in
the arts—" moft ignorant of what they're
moft affured"—who never felt any real
pleafure in his life, tho' he was ever
in fearch of it—This perfon remarking
the occupation of mind and cheerful air
of Adraftus, conceived that retirement
was the only plan for enjoyment, and
determined alfo to retire—which accordingly not long after he did, choofing
for his retreat a folitary place among the
lakes

lakes in Cumberland. Finding himſelf in a few minutes, very ſtupid; and in a few hours, the moſt miſerable of mortals, and conceiving ſome diſpleaſure againſt Adraſtus, by whoſe example he had been miſled; he very prudently determined to reſume his former mode of life, but in his way back to call on Adraſtus. Being at Brecon directed to his cottage, they had the following converſation—

C. The laſt time we met was on that mountain—do you recollect me, Sir?

A. I dare ſay I ſhall ſoon—an acquaintance begun on a mountain, with me is a ſacred thing—it is not like an introduction at a formal viſit.

C. I ſee that you have ſtill that cheerfulneſs which led me firſt to imagine it was your retirement that produced ſuch happy effects—in conſequence, I alſo retired—with much difficulty I held out

U 3   one

one day; and on the next, if I had not
left my difmal folitary cell I muſt have
ſent to the next town for a cord or a
piſtol.—You fairly took me in.

A. Admirable! a perſon like you acquainted with the world (for ſo I ſuppoſe) muſt often have heard that there is
no truſting to appearances—perhaps I am
a cheat—but I will not deceive you—I
really am as I appear—your miſtake was
in thinking that you and I are beings of
the ſame claſs—What ſays the poet?
" Man differs more from man, than man
from beaſt."

C. This is certain, that *I* find no
pleaſure in ſolitude, *you* do.

A. You again miſtake—ſolitude is to
me the moſt dreadful of all ideas—for
which reaſon I am never alone.

C.

C. Then I was mifinformed—

A. I confefs, appearances are againft me, but, to quote another poet—

" And this my life, exempt from public haunt,
Finds tongues in trees, books in the running brooks,
Sermons in ftones, and good in every thing."

Whatever I fee and hear is to me a fubject of amufement, delight, or inftruction; which perhaps is more than I fhould receive if I fought either from what is called fociety. The works of nature, confidered by themfelves, are a perpetual fource of entertainment to a mind in the habit of obfervation—to a *cultivated* mind, great pleafure arifes, from calling up remembrance of paffages in poets, which apply to the objects before you; and when we are reading thefe paffages, in referring them to the object or circumftance which firft infpired them. The fame mutual reference applies to painting. We trace in nature the fcenes which fired the ima-

U 4   gination

gination of Salvator, Pouffin, or Ruyf-
dael; and the pictures themfelves remind
us of that affemblage of objects to which
we owe thofe divine exertions of genius.
Where thefe fail, not an infect, or even
ftone, but may be confidered as a fubject
of difquifition in natural-hiftory or philofophy.—Do you call this folitude? Am
I not always in good company?

C. You have a particular turn—all
this is nothing to *me*—but fuppofe the
weather be unfavourable, and you cannot
go out?

A. Look on thefe fhelves—they contain about fifty volumes of the choiceft
Englifh, French, and Italian authors. In
that port-folio are fome drawings of the
beft artifts—and fee—there is a pile of
mufic-books, and an excellent piano-
forte.—Is this folitude?

C.

C. I have no relifh for reading, painting, or mufic—that is, in *your* way. I
like a newfpaper at my breakfaft—pictures are delightful at the exhibition,
when the room is full of company ; and
if I wifh for mufic I go to the Opera, and
there too the company is my chief in-
ducement—I am not particular—all people of tafte agree with me, and fo does
an old verfe-maker:

    " Let bear or elephant be e'er fo white,
    The *people*, fure the *people*, are the fight."

A. But, with thefe ideas in your head,
how could you think of living by yourfelf? If it will not punifh you too much,
permit me to read you a few thoughts on
retirement, which I committed to paper
the laft wet day—fome paffages are not
inapplicable to yourfelf, although the
fubject be on the propriety of retirement
for perfons advanced in life, which certainly is not your cafe—Have I your per-
miffion ?

                          C.

C. You will oblige me.

A. There is not a great deal of it—
(reading) The idea of young perfons re-
tiring from the world is too abfurd to be
made a queftion; but there are ftrong
reafons for the retirement of old perfons;
and, indeed, there are powerful arguments againft it.

Thofe who believe a preparation for
death to be neceffary, and think it of
confequence to keep their thoughts undifturbed by the affairs of the world,
fhould have nothing to interrupt their
meditations.

If we have lived a bufy life, and enjoyed a reputation for brilliant parts or
perfonal accomplifhments; the confcioufnefs of thofe faculties decaying may mor-
tify our confequence, and be a perpetual
fource of difguft if we ftill continue to
mix with the world.

Although

Although the body muft droop and fade, yet, if the mind enjoy its priftine vigour, retirement prevents occafions of expofing the decay of our perfonal faculties, and affords opportunities of enjoying mental pleafures, perhaps in a fuperior degree; as from experience we may have learnt to make a proper eftimate of ourfelves, of men, and their opinions: and knowing that thefe enjoyments are all that we have left, we value them as our fole poffeffions.

Retirement alfo puts in our power what remains of life, undifturbed, and unbroken by the interruptions of thofe, who, having no purfuit nor employment of their own, feem fent into world "to take us from ourfelves"—thefe reafons apply folely to perfons who have fomething to engage their thoughts and attention, and can derive entertainment and enjoyment from their own proper fources.

C.

C. Meaning *yourself*.

A. But for thofe of a contrary defcription, retirement is altogether improper—

C. Meaning *me*.

A. Such people fhould ftill continue
their worldly parfuits and employments ;
as they are, from habit, and want of mental
occupations, incapable of any other. Let
the tradefman then, whofe life has been
long in the fame courfe of employment,
ftill purfue his bufinefs, although his
fortune be far fuperior to his wants and
expences—retirement to him is mifery.

C. Right, right—

A. Thofe who have fpent their youth
in diffipation are conftrained to perfift in
the fame courfe, or to do nothing—the
moft difagreeable ftate of all others.

From

From this confideration I am much more inclined to pity, than to blame, perfons of the other fex, who to avoid vacancy, ftill continue to haunt places of gay refort, " and tho' they cannot play, o'er-look the cards." Retirement then, is only for thofe who find in *themfelves* amufement, employment, or happinefs. —And thus ends my fermon.

C. And my vifit—adieu !

The Reſtraint of Society.

ADRASTUS, tho' left " to purſue his vagaries in peace," as we have already remarked, yet many attempted to ſeek his acquaintance — ſome, becauſe they thought him an oddity; ſome, becauſe they thought him ſenſible; but moſt, becauſe they ſaw he ſhunned all advances towards intimacy: for mankind has a natural propenſity to teaze peculiar characters, even if the peculiarity be innocent. However, he contrived, by his perſeverance, to carry his point, and by his prudence to avoid offence.

The want of a few neceſſaries directed his ſteps to Brecon one fine morning, which, as cuſtomary in a mountainous country, becoming a rainy day, he dined

at

at the inn with a variety of ſtrangers, whoſe converſation chiefly turned upon the ſpirit of liberty which had broke forth of late in different parts of the world. Perſons who live in ſociety, and are in habits of converſation, never make long ſpeeches, from a principle of politeneſs, and ſoon exhauſt all they have to ſay upon a ſubject. The reverſe takes place with the recluſe—he having but few opportunities of converſation, indulges thoſe few when they occur; and having treaſured up a large ſtore of matter, makes an oſtentatious diſplay of his riches. Adraſtus, without duly reflecting on the laws of converſation, at laſt had all the diſcourſe to himſelf, and gave a turn to his oration on liberty, as new as it was unexpected— he expreſſed himſelf as follows :—

" There is no ſubject of late has more agitated the minds of men than liberty; upon the bleſſing of which they agree, although they materially differ upon the

means

means of obtaining it. However, all seem to limit their enquiries to what *form of government* liberty is most truly attached, and when they have determined the form agreeable to their own ideas, they seek no farther, conceiving the point to be established.

The enjoyment of liberty under an absolute prince seems so much like a contradiction, that blame may be incurred for even mentioning them together. It may be had under a limited monarchy, say the English; it is better obtained by a Republic and President, say the Americans; but it is best of all enjoyed when every man is a citizen, and no more than a citizen,* say the French; who are not contented with having it in this form themselves, but they seem determined that all the rest of the world shall be of their opinion. Thus Mahomet, thoroughly

* Written in 1793.

roughly perfuaded of the truth and fuperior goodnefs of his Koran, conceived it
a duty to propagate his doctrine by con-
queft. Thus the fanatics of the laft
century

 * * * " prov'd their doctrines orthodox
 By apoftolic blows and knocks"—

And thus the Catholics of all times, except the modern, thought they were doing
God and his Son good fervice, by forcing
a belief of chriftianity by the means of
tortures and death—hitherto *religious* opinions only have been thought worthy of
fuch great exertions, but our good neighbours have made *politics* of equal importance.

As a man is not fed by hearing of good
dinners, but by what he puts into his
own ftomach, fo, it may be prefumed,
no one feels the enjoyment of liberty farther than that portion which comes to
his own fhare. The reverfe of the po-

    X   fition

fition is equally true—if a man's perfon and actions are free, he enjoys liberty even under a defpot, but if his perfon or his actions are confined, he is a flave although a member of a Republic. Admitting the truth of this pofition; if circumftances in private life take our liberty from us, what are we the better for living under a free goverment; or how are we hurt by defpotifm if we may go, act, and fpeak as we pleafe?

Should it be faid, that the effence of a free government is to give liberty, and that the nature of defpotifm is to take it away; I can fubfcribe to this opinion no farther than it is true—and its truth only reaches to purpofes and occafions which do not occur in daily life, while either form of government leaves the flavery unremedied with which we are daily environed. If we are engaged in a lawfuit, or called to anfwer for fome offence, then we feel the advantage of a free go-

vernment

vernment with fixed laws, over a fentence pronounced by an arbitrary judge, appointed by an arbitrary mafter—but moft men pafs their days without going to law, and not one in fifty thoufand becomes a victim to juftice.

The real flavery we feel, and it is equal under all governments, is the reftraint of fociety; under which we are more compleatly fhackled in all our actions, words, and even thoughts, than by the moft imperious commands of the moft abfolute tyrant—for a defpotic mandate does not defcend to minute particulars; it puts on a chain, but leaves fome limbs at liberty; while the tyranny of fociety draws a thoufand flender threads over us from head to foot, by which we are more compleatly hampered than Gulliver in Lilliput.

I can fcarce flatter myfelf to have proceeded thus far without incurring fome.

cenfure,

cenfure, nor to finifh my fubject, without more. I certainly might, without
trefpafs, have walked in a beaten path,
which if I quit, it muft be to my own
peril—I tremble while I fay—that the
marriage-vow—the reciprocal duty between parents and children—the offices
of friendfhip—the ceremonies of civility
—all thefe take from us more perfonal
liberty than can be ballanced by any po-
litical liberty which the moft perfect
form of government can beftow.

Should you think that more pleafure
arifes from fuch reftraints than without
them—be it fo; but do not fay they are
confiftent with liberty. If a father gives
up his own enjoyment to encreafe that of
a fon—if a fon abridges his own pleafures
becaufe he will not violate his duty to a
parent—if my friend has my money, and
I want it myfelf—if my time, inftead of
being my own, is confumed in attentions
to acquaintance and the ceremonies of
company

company—all thefe circumftances may perhaps encreafe our enjcyment, but they furely diminifh our liberty. The more we feel an *obligation* to do an action, the more is the choice taken from us of doing it, or not, as we pleafe; of courfe, the more is our liberty abridged. If nature, cuftom, or the rules of fociety *require* us to fulfil certain duties to our relations, friends, or acquaintance; our not having it in our power to act otherwife is certainly the definition of real flavery.

Let not my intention be miftaken. I am not fpeaking againft natural or focial attachments; my opinion of them perfectly agrees with the reft of the world— I only attempt to prove, that our greateft reftraints do not arife from defpotifm in any form of government, but from ourfelves. " We complain of our taxes," fays Dr. Franklyn, " we tax ourfelves more than we can be taxed by a Minifter." It is our *private* habits by which we are

affected

affected—in the common duties of fociety is a greater portion of flavery than can be inflicted by the moft defpotic fovereign."

The rapidity with which this fatirical oration was delivered, did not permit a fingle word to be thruft in by way of interruption—but no fooner was it concluded, than the company made amends for their retention, by all fpeaking together; fome to commend, but moft to object. Adraftus being truly fenfible of his indifcretion, with great difpatch paid for his ordinary, and left the company to cut up his argument as a defert to their dinner.

On

On Rhyme.

RHYME is allowed not to have exifted until after the claffical ages, on which account it is held by fome to be barbarous; others think it fo congenial with modern languages, that our poetry cannot fubfift without it—Milton feems to have been of the former opinion, and Dr. Johnfon of the latter.

On this fubject, as well as many others, we fhould form rules from authorized practice, and not force great geniufes to fubmit to our regulations. Poffeffing fo much exquifite poetry in rhyme, let us not call rhyme barbarous; and when reading Milton and Shakefpeare, can we fay that rhyme is *effential* to poetry? From the effect of rhyme and blank-

X 4   verfe,

verfe, when ufed by good poets, we may
venture upon fome diftinctions, although
we dare not make laws.

When we read the Iliad by Pope, and
the Paradife Loft, we are ready to pronounce, from their difference, that long
poems ought to be in blank verfe :* and
fhort ones, being conftantly in rhyme,
(with a very few exceptions) we may be
affured that they ought to be fo. There
is certainly a difference of character between long and fhort pieces—a poem of
length is not many fhort ones put together, nor will a fmall part of a long poem
make a fhort one. Take any detached
part of the Paradife Loft, however beautiful, yet it evidently belongs to fome
great whole ; whereas a fhort piece has
the

---

* The Lycidas and Samfon Agoniftes of Milton
have rhymes in a fcattered irregular manner, which
is a very pleafing ftructure for a poem of length—
it gives a connection of parts without the conftant
artificial return of the ftanza or couplet.

the air of fomething begun, and concluded, in a few lines. There is a greatnefs
of defign and a breadth of pencilling in
the one—a neatnefs of touch and high-
finifhing in the other. In fome very few
inftances both thefe qualities are united:
Hudibras and the Alma, although poems
of length, have all the point of epigram.
If then high-finifhing and neatnefs be
characteriftics of fhort pieces, it accounts
for rhyme being fo effential to their perfection—blank verfe, as before obferved,
belongs to fomething large in defign and
manner. Another effential of fmall poems
is, that the conclufion fhould have fomething to mark it. As I have mentioned
this more at large elfewhere, I fhall only
here remark, that Horace's Odes in general are deficient in this particular, and
that the fhort pieces of Voltaire never
want it.

Another effect of rhyme is, connecting
the parts of the poem, as far as the ftruc-

ture

ture is concerned. To fhew the good effects of this connection was the occafion of the above prefatory remarks; and, by reducing it to a figure, perhaps we may have a rule for judging of the merit of different difpofitions of rhyme in the various fpecies of poetry.

A piece compofed of couplets may be exprefled thus

$$
\left.\begin{array}{l}
- \ - \ - \ - \ - \ - \ - \ - \ a \\
- \ - \ - \ - \ - \ - \ - \ - \ a
\end{array}\right)
$$
$$
\left.\begin{array}{l}
- \ - \ - \ - \ - \ - \ - \ - \ o \\
- \ - \ - \ - \ - \ - \ - \ - \ o
\end{array}\right)
$$

which has the appearance of two things joined together, or one divided into halves.

The alternate rhyme—thus—

Here the lines are fo connected, that the firſt two cannot fubfiſt without the two laſt; therefore the four lines make a whole. But if a long piece were fo conſtructed, each quatrain would appear one fingle unconnected thing, and have a worſe effect than the couplet.

There is yet another difpofition of four lines

which does better for long pieces, and worfe for ſhort.

The ſtanza of fix, feven, eight, and nine lines, is varioufly compofed, and fometimes very artfully; but its merit altogether confiſts, as far as relates to ſtructure, in a proper connection and variety

riety of the rhymes—let us exprefs a few
of them

ufed by an unknown author in a fine
poem on his birth-day.

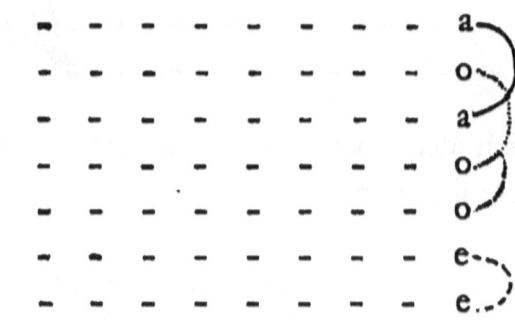

The above is Chaucer's Stanza, which
has not an ill effect—the difconnected
couplet rather gives a precifion and finifh
to the ftanza, and would be an exception

tion to the rule, if its conftant return had not in fome. meafure the effect of con-nection.

In Spencer's and Beattie's Stanza the lines are thus connected.

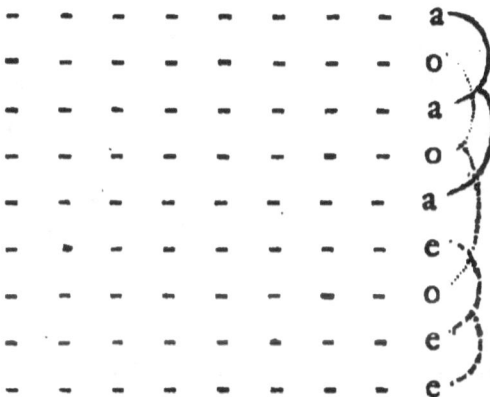

The rhymes in all ftanzas of this kind are finely difpofed for connection, and the whole is tyed together fo effectually, that the lines cannot be disjoined from each other. If the ftanza had confifted of couplets, the lines might have been feparated into pairs.

From

From the above obfervations it does not feem difficult to determine, whether the legitimate Sonnet of Petrarch, and his numberlefs fucceffors, has any advantage over the modern little poem, confifting, like its original, of fourteen lines, but the rhymes difpofed at pleafure. All rules which do not tend to produce good effect " are more honoured in the breach than the obfervance." But if it be a point of perfection that the parts of a fhort poem fhould be connected, and not capable of difunion; it will be found that the old fonnet poffeffes this perfection, and that the modern wants it.

Petrarch and his imitators, Spencer and Milton, generally connected their lines in this manner.

I

```
 1  -  -  -  -  -  -  a
 2  -  -  -  -  -  -  o
 3  -  -  -  -  -  -  o
 4  -  -  -  -  -  -  a
 5  -  -  -  -  -  -  a
 6  -  -  -  -  -  -  o
 7  -  -  -  -  -  -  o
 8  -  -  -  -  -  -  a

                    *

 9  -  -  -  -  -  -  e
10  -  -  -  -  -  -  i
11  -  -  -  -  -  -  u
12  -  -  -  -  -  -  e
13  -  -  -  -  -  -  i
14  -  -  -  -  -  -  u
```

The irregular fonnet fometimes confifts of couplets, ufually of quatrains, either in alternate rhyme or otherwife; fo
that although the thought may be fimple,
and run through the whole, yet the ftructure confifts of diftinct parts, fucceeding
each

* At this break the rhymes begin upon a new
fyftem.

each other—this may be eafily conceived after the preceding illuftrations. The one poffeffing union, and the other wanting it, undoubtedly determines the point in favour of the old fonnet. It muft be obferved, (although it has been hinted already,) that when we ufe the terms connection, &c. that they relate entirely to the form, and not to the fubject—a piece may be disjoined in its ftructure, but entire in its fubject, which may prevent the difconnection from being obferved; but if the lines are tyed together, we perceive the effect increafed, as the fonnet is one in its thought and expreffion. Thefe irregular little pieces fhould have fome appropriate term, becaufe the old-form of a fonnet feems as effential as its confifting of fourteen lines.*

Perhaps

---

* It is not altogether foreign to the fubject, to remark, that in Chaucer a paragraph often ends with a half-couplet; which is ftill the cuftom of

the

Perhaps the above obfervations may furnifh a principle for determining the refpective merit of the different kinds of poetry. If it be admitted—blank-verfe is better than rhyme for long works— rhyme better than blank-verfe for fhort pieces—alternate rhyme beft for the qua-train‡ ; and the fixed form of the ancient fonnet, is to be preferred to the irregular ftructure of that poem to which the mo-derns have affixèd the fame appellation.

the French poets. It certainly has an unpleafing effect, as the fenfe and the rhyme do not conclude together, but the compleating of the couplet con-nects the prefent paragraph with the paft.

‡ This word is affumed to fave the trouble of frequently ufing the long term of The four-line ftanza.

Y   On

Odd Numbers.

THAT there fhould be fome general principles which are common to all men, is eafily conceived—but it feems difficult to affign a reafon why diftinct nations, having no connection with each other, fhould agree in fome odd peculiarity.

To thofe people who are acquainted with numeration beyond the ends of their ten fingers, it feems moft natural, that whole numbers fhould be employed for general purpofes. Thus we make prizes of £.1000 or £.10,000 in the lottery, rather than 999 or 9999. But if we had chofen the odd numbers, there would have been inftances enough to be found in different parts of the world, and even among ourfelves, to keep us in countenance.

nance. Take a few as they occur, which
might be much increafed from accounts
of the manners and cuftoms of different
nations.

" The Mandingoes (an African nation)
according to a precept of the Alcoran, limit the number of ftripes for fmall crimes
to forty lacking one, and for greater of-
fences to ninety and nine." (Mathews.)
St. Paul fays, he received forty ftripes
fave one. A flave in the Weft-Indies is
alfo punifhed with forty fave one. On
board our fhips of war all punifhments of
this fort were formerly inflicted in odd
numbers: they gave (as they term it) a
merry eleven; and for greater faults, two
or three merry elevens—whether this
agrees with the prefent difcipline I know
not.

The game of cribbage is 101—if I die
(fay the common people) within a twelve-
month and a day.

There

There are 999 fish-ponds within the walls of Nankin. The Emperor of China has 9999 boats. The number of idols in a Temple at Jedo, the capital of Japan, Thunberg tells us, is 33333. With the last number we have nothing to compare, but let us not forget our leafes for 999 years.

Why people so different in manners, and distant in situation, should agree in this peculiarity, which surely is the reverse of a general principle; or why 11, 39, 99, 999, or lastly 33333, should be preferred to the even numbers which stand next them, and have so superior a claim, requires more skill, than I possess, to explain.

Is it superstition? If so, are all people superstitious, and in the same particular? —The first may be admitted, but not the latter—the same principle, in other instances, is various in its operation. Perhaps

haps an oddity of this fort, although found in a civilized nation, had its firſt origin when it was barbarous. As civilization makes all nations uniform, ſo the want of it may produce a ſameneſs of character between people remote from each other. It is in the early ſtages of ſociety that ſuch whimſies make their firſt appearance. But this ſubject makes part of another which I have before treated at large.*

* In the Four Ages.

Late.

Late.

THE manners of the prefent age may be characterized by one fhort word, *Late.* Whatever hour is fixed for an engagement of any fort, it is never kept. If you invite your guefts at five, they come at fix—if a public entertainment begins at feven, you leave your houfe at eight. This practice is inconvenient even in trifles, but in things of confequence, it is thoroughly reprehenfible. It was no lefs truly than wittily faid, by Lord Chefterfield, of the old Duke of Newcaftle— " His Grace lofes an hour in the morning, and is looking for it all the reft of the day."

Perhaps the real fource of our want of fuccefs with a vigilant and *punctual* ene-

my,

my, is protracting the time for action—not confidering, that according to the proverb, it ftays for no man, and that if we are too late, it fignifies not whether it be by a minute or a year.

In the American war many wife and brilliant plans were adopted, which had no other fault than being *too late*—we had the victory to gain, when we ought to have been enjoying the fruits of it. The laft public inftance of this deftructive principle (at the time of writing this) was in the failing of the Channel fleet, which, by lofing a fortnight, moft probably will occafion a train of misfortune which diftant ages may not recover. Whatever virtues the prefent Miniftry may poffefs, they are more than balanced by this pernicious *monofyllable*; and as there is not the leaft reafon for fuppofing that the members of oppofition have more punctuality, we fhould gain nothing by an exchange.

Y 4 The

The following anecdote would be ridiculous, if the caufe of it did not make part of all our concerns, either in private or public life. An appointment was made with an aftronomer to be at his obfervatory to fee an eclipfe. The good company confidering cœleftial and terreftrial engagements in the fame light, attended the philofopher, and after chatting for fome time, at laft recollected their bufinefs, and begged to fee the eclipfe—I am forry, fays the Doctor, that I could not prevail on the fun and moon to wait for you—the eclipfe was ended long before your arrival.

HASSAN of Shiraz poffeffing wealth, which he rafhly deemed inexhauftible, became the flave of pleafure. Tartarian females were employed by turns in fanning him through the night, and, at times, fprinkling his fkin with rofewater. Ice-fruits and coftly comfitures were his morning regale, which being ended, he bathed in polifhed bafons of white marble, and inhaled the breeze of fragrance from the Jafmins of Arabia. Borne by his fervants in a ftately litter to the Bazar, he paffed flowly before the fhops of the artificers, looking with a languid, but curious eye, on their various productions of ingenuity; endeavouring to find a want, or to create a wifh—but his wants and wifhes had been too often

fupplied

fupplied to be ftill importunate. The
workers in filligree and embroidery, the
carvers in ivory, the goldfmiths, the
jewellers, had nothing to engage his attention. The Armenian merchants, indeed, would fhew him, in fecret, the
coftly works of the Franguis, pictures
exhibiting refemblances of human figures,
which, becaufe they are forbidden by our
law, he eagerly purchafed. On his return, ftopping where provifions are fold,
he ordered a fumptuous fupper to regale
his numerous friends, who never failed
to affociate at his entertainment, quaffing,
in cups of chriftal, the delicious liquor
which the holy prophet commands us not
to drink, while troops of dancers and
jugglers, fucceeding each other, furnifhed
the paffing moments with delight.

Having no fource of employment from
his own mind, he found himfelf conftrained to continue his diffipation, to
avoid that frightful ftate of vacancy felt

by

by all who depend upon external circumstances for pleafure. The wealth of the Khan of Shiraz was too little to fupply his conftant expences. When his laft Toman was fpent; afhamed to continue in poverty where he had lived in fplendor, he wandered from the city over the plain without direction, as his wifh was rather to avoid his home than to reach any other place.

Evening approached; the ftately mofques of Shiraz were vanifhing in aerial obfcurity, but no other town opened on his view; and as he had not compleated a ufual day's journey, even the folitary caravan-ferai was wanting to give him fhelter and repofe.

The cold dews of night moiftened his turban, and ftood in drops upon his cangiar and fcymetar, when he heard in the mountains not far diftant, the barking of jackalls, the howling of hyænas, and the
roaring

roaring of the mighty tyger; for now was the time when the wild-beasts of the forest assume their turn to reign—the day they give up to man.

Fear of immediate danger banished from his mind the regret for having spent his substance—displaced the horror of finding himself without companions, upon whom had rested his sole dependance to fill up the frightful void of life—and even prevented his attending to the calls of hunger; a sensation, which, until this day, he had never felt. " There is no other God but one—Mahomet is his prophet!" said he earnestly, for the first time with *devotion*—before the hour of danger, it had only been his *custom* when the crier from the Minaret called the faithful to prayer.

The wandering fires which nightly flit across the plain, to the accustomed traveller are objects of amusement, to Haf-

fan

ſan they were ſights of terror: yet he
followed them with his eye, and, by degrees, with his feet, until he had deviated from the road which had brought him
from Schiraz.—Diſmal reflections occurred in comparing his preſent ſituation
with that of the preceding evening, when
the ſounds and lights were thoſe of mirth
and feſtivity.

While he was reſting, without a motive to retire or advance, he heard a creak-
ing noiſe juſt before him, which was
followed by a man ariſing from the earth
with a taper in his hand, who preſently
ſhut the trap-door from whence he had
aſcended. Unconſcious of being obſerved,
he advanced where Haſſan was ſtanding,
and ſtarted back at the reflection from the
ſcymetar, drawn by Haſſan on the firſt
impulſe of fear. " Alas!" ſaid the ſtranger, " I am diſcovered—do not take the
life of one diſarmed, and who has not offended." " Thy life," replied Haſſan,
" I

" I cannot take, unlefs the angel of death permits; and, if thy moments are exhaufted, thou canft not by entreaties add to their number. I am a traveller who feeks fhelter and repofe—if thy habitation is near, conduct me to it."

The ftranger fearing the fcymetar of Haffan, returned to the trap-door— " Follow me," fays he, defcending— " my abode is contrary to that of other mortals—they live *upon* the earth, I *under* it." Haffan, who had never feen any apartments but thofe of magnificence; as he furveyed afkance the gloomy paffages, felt that he had only changed one terror for another.

They, at laft, entered a fpacious arched hall, nearly full of coffers and bags, arranged round the walls, and which left but a fmall fpace for the owner and his gueft.

Haffan,

Haffan, now protected by the laws of hofpitality, fheathed his fcymetar, while his hoft put on the table two fmall loaves, fome grapes, and a veffel of the amber wine of Shiraz. " Eat and refrefh your-felf," fays Dahir (the owner of the cave) " I have fupped already, and cannot eat with you, being about to depart for Shi-raz, where I go twice or thrice in a week to renew my ftock of provifion—I always travel by night for fear of difcovery ; but as you are now as much in *my* power as I at firft was in *yours*, let mutual confidence fucceed to mutual fears."

H. As I am in your power, and pro-mife you fidelity, I may afk an expla-nation of appearances which at prefent puzzle me.

D. Thofe coffers and bags you fee are all full of coined gold from our early em-perors to Schah Abbas—the accumulation of five generations ! They are here de-pofited posited as in a place of safety against the rapacity of the Khan of Schiraz or his Minifters.

H. They are, perhaps, in safety, but are of no use—if your coffers contained only earth, it would be of equal value to riches not used.

D. The value of a thing is in proportion to the happinefs it beftows. If my coffers were only full of earth they would give me no pleafure, but I receive much from reflecting that they are full of gold.

H. How you can receive any when your money is not beftowed, is paft my conception. Pleafure may be purchafed —as I know to my coft.

D. To your coft? Then I fuppofe *your* plan was fpending your money—has it led you to happinefs?

H.

H. I cannot fay it has—my mifery is extreme!

D. Very well; now, mark the difference between us. I have pleafure in furveying my chefts—I count them—I fometimes regale my eyes by looking at my money—after which I lock it up, and reflect, that the means of procuring every thing are in my power—but if I part with my gold, I then lofe the means and the pleafure of the reflection.

H. But do you never intend to ufe your money?

D. I at prefent ufe it to the beft of purpofes—to give me happinefs; but if I fpent it, I fhould have none. How can you be fo obftinate to continue a difpute, when you confefs that a conduct contrary to mine has led you to mifery?

Z   Haffan

Haffan was filent, but not convinced; fo deep had the common opinion of the ufe of riches funk within his mind— " But, pray," fays he, " may not happinefs be found in fomething between both our fyftems?"

" I do not want," replied Dahir, " to confine happinefs in one path: all I contend for is, that I feel it myfelf— you certainly are at liberty to feek happinefs wherever it may be found. But what can I do with you? Here you cannot ftay, and if you go you will difcover my treafure—fwear to me by the head of the prophet, that you will come here no more, and I will take the fame oath to fend you a camel-load of my gold —it is better to part with fome than lofe the whole.

The mutual oath was fworn, and at day-break Haffan returned to the city.

The

The gold was fent according to promife, together with a roll of perfumed
paper, beautifully embellifhed, on which
was written in elegant characters—

" Haffan, oppofe not thy particular
opinion to the general fyftem of the moft
high! Various are the fituations in life,
and all concur to fulfill the decrees of
eternal wifdom. *The ufe of accumulation
is to repair the wafte of prodigality.*"

On

HAVING for fome time heard nothing
of the Robin-Hood Society, perhaps it
ceafes to exift; if fo, the public has to
regret the cheapeft fchool for oratory ever
inftituted. Many a Templar would have
been dafhed at his firft motion in Weft-
minfter-Hall, but for the opportunity
this fociety afforded for trying the fteadi-
nefs of his face, and the ftrength of his
voice. Many a youth, who has fince fupported or oppofed the Minifter, here firft
made effay of his talent for affertion or
contradiction, and learnt to bear, without
being interrupted, the cheering founds
" Hear him! hear him!"

Whatever may have become of this
learned feminary of eloquence, there ftill
exifts

exifts (if not deftroyed by a late law) eftablifhments for the ufeful purpofe of mending our decayed Conftitution, where a young beginner may ftudy what effect his voice may have on himfelf and auditory. It is rather an hazardous undertaking for a perfon to fpeak contrary to the fenfe of his hearers, as he may not, (tho' ever fo faithful) get off with flying colours like Abdiel; yet, a rafh youth, depending upon liberal treatment, where liberty was fuppofed to be the firft principle of a popular club, ventured thus to addrefs his audience—

Mr. PRESIDENT,

There are many focieties, befides this, in the kingdom, that have for their object a Reform of Parliament, and it feems to be the intention of Miniftry to oppofe this Reform. If I am not intimidated by this refpectable affembly of patriots, from expreffing and connecting my ideas, I

Z 3　　　　　hope

hope to fhew, that if the focieties attain
their purpofe, no better meafures would
be purfued than at prefent; and that the
Miniftry might grant their defire without
lofing any of the influence they would
wifh to obtain over the Parliament.

It is confeffed by all parties, that there
are many boroughs reprefented that are
without fufficient confequence, and many
places which ought to fend members, un-
reprefented—that the mode of election,
and the electors themfelves, are exceptionable.—If this be granted, then why
not reform? I have not the leaft objection—fuppofe it done—

A Parliament is now affembled, to
which every place that ought, has fent
members; and every place that ought
not, has fent none. Not only freemen
and freeholders, but all men, women,
and children, have united in their choice,
without one diffentient voice—I think,
Mr.

Mr. Prefident, I have made a Houfe of Commons more perfect than even the moſt ſanguine reformers have yet pro-jected. Now, if ever, the ſenſe of the people will be declared in the Houſe, and, as it ought, govern every thing. *(Ap-plauſes.)* But, Sir, not to be loſt in a crowd of five hundred perſons, let us take one ſingle repreſentative, and ſee firſt, whether the people have made a proper choice; and, ſuppoſing it made, whether there is a poſſibility of his ſpeak-ing the ſenſe of his conſtituents.

Let us imagine a town in which are ſome virtuous citizens occupied in their profeſſions, or in literary purſuits. Know-ing the value of their time, they do not throw it away, but employ it for ſome honourable or profitable purpoſe, by which they are to become richer, wiſer, or better. Such perſons are of no eſti-mation in the eyes of the vulgar—they have no glitter to attract their notice.

But

But if there be within their obfervation, a 'Squire Weftern, who loves his dogs and his bottle, who confumes his time in idlenefs and diffipation; they confider him as a hearty fellow—a jolly dog, and of courfe has the good-fortune to win their hearts.

A new Parliament is to be chofen— Where will the people look for a repre- fentative? Not in their own town, but at the refidence of their favourite—for, fay they, this man is of family and for- tune, therefore he has confequence, and is above being influenced—this may be true, but ftill he wants a principal qualifica- tion—knowledge of the duty of a fenator. The utmoft that can be expected is, that he is too ignorant to do harm.

But admitting his abilities—a queftion comes on in the houfe—" Shall there be war or peace !"—His private opinion is for war, and that is alfo the wifh of many

of

of his conftituents; but there are many others, perhaps the greater part, who are for peace. He votes according to his own opinion, by which the majority of his conftituents are, in this cafe, un‐reprefented: (indeed the laft obfervation is equally true in all reprefentative affem‐blies). Multiply this fingle inftance by 534, and you have a compleat idea what a Houfe of Commons would be, fo chofen.

How it ever could get into the imagi‐nation of a fenfible man, that the people have a better judgement of integrity or abilities, than perfons of education and honour, is difficult to conceive. Suppo‐fing the common-people impoffible to be influenced, the reverfe of which, is the fact; what reafon can be affigned why their choice fhould be preferred, where they are incapable of judging? *(Murmurs of difapprobation)* I am perfectly fenfible that the head to contrive would fignify nothing, unlefs there be hands to exe‐
cute,

cute, and that the people are thefe hands
(Bravo, bravo!)—But, if you difturb the
order, and convert the hands into the
head, your work can neither be contrived
nor executed. If a painter were ever fo
fkilful he could do nothing without the
colourman, nor could the organift without the bellows-blower. But does it
therefore follow that the colourman and
bellows-blower are judges of painting and
mufic? Is it not a fimilar argument to
fay, that tho' it is from the labour of the
people that we are maintained, that our
taxes are paid, and that the means of our
commerce are produced; yet, if you take
them from this their proper ftation, they
not only lofe their confequence, but
would, as well as their fuperiors, foon
lofe their exiftence. In fhort, it is for
the intereft of the whole together, and
of feparate individuals as well, (without
which general intereft is but a name) that
the people do not become governors.
The old fable of the Belly and Members
has

has fomewhat of this application. *(Symptoms of impatience; but the orator not daunted, proceeded).*

I cannot fancy that the House of Commons would confift of better perfons, tho' chofen in proportion to the confequence of the place—for Mr. Pitt or Mr. Fox would be as honeft and as eloquent whether they reprefented a Cornifh borough, or the metropolis. Neither can I fuppofe that any House of Commons is out of the influence of a minifter who has fo much to beftow. *(Applaufe.)* If a man is to be bought, he is as obnoxious to a bribe, tho' chofen by the fwinifh herd (a term I much approve) as if - - - - *(Off, off, off, down with him, down, down!)*

Mr. President,

No difputant can ever wifh for a more fortunate circumftance than when he can

make

make his adverfary to anfwer himfelf
(Off, off.) (Prefident. *Hear him!*) I
thank you, Sir—a certain perfon hoftile
to our principles; as we all know, compared the people to an herd of fwine—
Why? " Becaufe," fays he, " they go
as they are driven."—I make ufe of the
fame figure, becaufe, (as every hog-driver
will tell you) they go the *contrary* way
to that they are driven *(Ha, ha, ha!)*
therefore let not the allufion offend, but
fuffer me to proceed—

It is the nature of man to be dependent
where he cannot rule, and as all cannot
rule, fome muft be dependent. The
minifter is always confidered as the ruler
of a country; and thofe who are not
minifters, muft fubmit to be governed.
There is nothing got by refiftance—fuppofe the man in power turned out, fome
one elfe muft be put in—let monarchy
be deftroyed, fome other government
(and a miniftry in courfe) muft be eftablifhed

blifhed—fuppofe the moft perfect democracy; even then the power of government muft be given to a few individuals,
and one of thefe will govern. Whether
the government be in a king, an arifto-
cracy, or democracy; ftill whatever go-
verns muft be abfolute. The French
Directory is as abfolute as the French
Monarchy, with this difference in favour
of the latter—that redrefs of grievances
was eafier to be obtained.

If then the Houfe of Commons would
moft probably confift of the fame fort of
people as at prefent (where the change
was not for the worfe) it is fcarce worth
while to be very anxious for another mode
of electing reprefentatives—and, from the
fame confideration, the minifter need not
oppofe the wifh of the people for a reform (if they really have the wifh) for
he would find, as it is found at prefent,
that the Houfe of Commons will always
confift of a few of great abilities, a few
of

of fmall abilities, and the bulk; of middling people—of fome that will fupport, of others that will oppofe him, but the principal part muft always be as they ever have been, perfons more likely to follow than to lead, and whofe hands—I mean, whofe ears, are not always fhut to reafon."

The laft fentence being pronounced in rather a fly manner, made the audience conceive fomething of a joke was intended—while, looking at each other, they were puzzling to find it out; the orator defcended foftly from the roftrum, and, in as few fteps as poffible, happily efcaped into the ftreet.

On

*Authors should not exceed common judge-
ment.*

TO the many obstructions in the way
of fame, which I have elsewhere remarked, may be added another, of as
much force as any, or perhaps all of
them together.

If an author or artist be *too* clever, he
is as far from notice as if he were deficient. The science of success, is the
knowledge of what the world is *up to.*
This Oxford vulgarism so well expresses
my idea, that I shall use it for the present purpose.

A genius who is possessed of abilities
to carry his art *far* beyond the point to
which it has already attained, must be
very

very careful of fhewing thefe abilities.
As the public is not *up* to the judging of
them, they cannot diftinguifh what is
above their comprehenfion, from what is
beneath their notice. The common effect of this ignorance is, that the author
or artift, in order to live, muft let himfelf down to the level of the underftanding of thofe whom Fate has conftituted
his judges. If he be not impatient for
fame, he ought rather to elevate the public judgement to *him*, fo that it may be
competent to his productions. This conduct he feldom can purfue, and all the
good which might be obtained from fuperior abilities, is loft by the deficiency
of the public tafte, or the want of refolution (perhaps, want of bread) in the
artift.

This may poffibly account for the
wretched performances which difgrace
our theatres and places of public amufement. The like reafon has been affigned
why

why Shakefpeare fo frequently defcends below himfelf—it may be fo—I mean not to infinuate that he had fufficient tafte to lead him to rejeƈt abfurdities—but if he had poffeffed it, the want 'of tafte in the public would have fuppreffed his efforts towards correƈtnefs.

If you prefent to the public any produƈtion they are not *up to;* perfons who feel they know nothing, yet have the credit of knowing a great deal, inftantly abufe it to fhew their judgement; and difcover their ingenuity, by pointing out particular parts for difapprobation not apparent to the common eye. Others, who have no great reputation in the world, look vacant and fay nothing: but thofe who are efteemed wits, turn it to ridicule—and noify wit is more than a match for filent truth.

It is this want of knowledge in the public that is the real caufe why moft

A a   original

original geniufes are ftarved. The world is not malicious, but it cannot be faid to be interefted in the advancement of genius. The public is only indifferent in this affair, which indifference arifes from ignorance of the value of the thing.

Thefe reflections derive the bad fate of genius from a fource not mentioned in the Thirty Letters. Unfortunate for original merit, that there fhould be fuch a variety of caufes to hinder its advancement!

On the joining Poetry with Mufic.

IN fome late remarks* on a mufical publication, a wifh is expreffed, that the alliance of mufic and poetry were dif-folved. If by this is meant, that they are two diftinct things, and exift inde-pendently of each other, it cannot be doubted; but if it means, that they ought always to be kept afunder, or that they are not the ftronger from being properly united; the affertion, at leaft, may be queftioned.

When we read the Faery-Queene or Paradife-Loft, it is without the intrufion of any mufical idea; the poems might have been written if mufic had never ex-ifted,

A a 2

* In the Monthly Review.

ifted, for the meafure of the verfe, which is all the analogy that can be pretended, bears no relation to *mufical* meafure. Nay, thofe pieces which have lines of fuch a length as eafily coincide with equal bars, are written and read, without any reference to mufic.

In like manner, when we hear a fymphony, or any compofition merely inftrumental, it is unaccompanied by poetical ideas; the compofer thought of nothing but his fubject, and the audience do not affociate with it either verfe or profe—in this fenfe then, there is no natural union between poetry and mufic: but an artificial union may be formed, and with increafed effect. After we have been accuftomed to hear the fame words fung to a particular air, the latter, if heard alone, will weakly excite the fame kind of paffion as when performed together—but if the tune had never been applied to the words, no fuch paffion would have

have been excited, for mufic receives a determinate meaning from the words, which alone, it can never attain.* The fong and chorus of " Return O God of Hofts," in the Oratorio of Samfon, is undoubtedly a fine piece of devotional mufic, but it might with equal eafe have been adapted to the complaints of a lover for the lofs of his miftrefs. The old pfalm-tunes, fo expreffive of religious folemnity, were formerly in the French court applied to licentious fongs; and that peculiarly

---

* It is true that we find the terms *fummer* and *winter*, *noon* and *night*, *battle* and *chace*, given to pieces from fome fancied refemblance between them. The proving that fummer and winter, &c. have no connection with mufical expreffion, I fuppofe will not be expected. As marches are performed by military bands, they induce the idea of foldiers—when we hear *one* we think of the *other*; and as French-horns make part of the paraphernalia of hunting, in pieces where we find a frequent interchange of fifths, fixths, and octaves, we join with it the idea of a chace—but all this is affociation.

culiarly fine melody appropriated to the
hundredth pfalm, was fung to a popular
love-ditty. At prefent we may obferve
the reverfe—many of our favourite fong-
tunes, are, by fome religious eftablifhments, applied to their hymns; which,
as one of their teachers obferved, is ref-
cuing a good thing out of the clutches of
Satan. Thefe converfions could never
have fucceeded, if poetry had not the
power to determine what idea the mufic
fhould exprefs—take a yet ftronger inftance. Let us imagine ourfelves unacquainted with the well-known chorus of
" For unto us, &c." and that we heard
the inftrumental parts only—we fhould
think it a fugue upon a pleafing fubject,
without applying it to any particular
meaning, facred or prophane. Conceive
it part of a comic opera—nothing is more
eafy than preferving the fame form of
words in a parody, to fuit the purpofe—
fuppofe it done, and that there were
common names in place of the fublime
appellations

appellations of the original—they would be equally well expreſſed; perhaps in one part, better; for the ſpace between " called," and the name, is ſo filled up in the violin parts, as would more properly introduce the names we have imagined to be ſubſtituted, than thoſe terms which really follow.

Let us next ſuppoſe the compoſer of an oratorio applying the ſame muſic to the paſſage in the prophet, as at preſent, and the chorus is heard with its proper words. We have now a ſublime and religious idea impreſſed, to which we think the muſic admirably adapted, and where our ſenſation is in uniſon. Religion and ridicule differing in the extreme, no other ſubjects could be found ſo proper for proving the point to be eſtabliſhed.

By all theſe inſtances, it is plain, that the ſame muſic may be applied for oppoſite purpoſes, and equally well; and al-

though

though they alſo evidently ſhew that
muſic alone expreſſes no *determinate* ſen-
timent, yet that it increaſes the expreſſion, and even meaning of the words,
whenever they are judiciouſly conjoined;
for whether the muſic had been *only* applied to the pſalms or ſongs—to the cho-
ruſes either for a ſerious or comic effeẟ;
yet it is moſt certain that the words and
the muſic are the more expreſſive for
each other.

Let muſic and poetry then be kept
diſtinẟ, when it is for their mutual advantage to be ſo; they have each their
particular, and ſufficient conſequence, to
ſubſiſt, without collateral ſupport; but
all the world has felt that they may be
combined, and receive ſo much additional effeẟ, that we muſt oppoſe the
ſlighteſt wiſh to diſſolve an union pro-
duẟive of ſuch exquiſite pleaſure.

Almanacks.

Almanacks.

" THE ancient Saxons ufed to engrave
" upon certain fquare fticks about a foot
" in length, fhorter or longer as they
" pleafed, the courfes of the moons of
" the whole year, whereby they could
" always certainly tell when the new-
" moons, full-moons, and changes fhould
" happen; and fuch carved fticks they
" called Al-mon-aght, that is to fay,
" All-moon-heed; to wit, the regard or
" obfervation of all the moons; and hence
" is derived the name of Almanack."

VERSTEGAN.

This is a clear derivation of the term
Almanack, and fhews the miftake of
thofe who would derive it from the Ara-
bic, becaufe of the firft fyllable *Al*.

There

There is in St. John's College, Cambridge, a Saxon Almanack exactly answering to the above defcription; and I have in my poffeffion an Almanack made in the reign of Edward the Third, of parchment; not in the ufual form of a fheet, or a book, but in feparate pieces, folded in the fhape of a flat flick or lath, in the Saxon fafhion. It is perfectly fair, and exhibits the beft fpecimen of the ancient numerals I have yet met with.

The method of beginning and dividing the year, as in our Almanacks, is barbarous enough, but might eafily be reformed. There are, no doubt, numberlefs objections to the difturbing a fixed method of reckoning time; but if a new form muft be adopted, I would recommend, as a model, the druidical year, which commenced at the winter folftice, when the days having gone through their total increafe and decreafe, begin their courfe anew. Thefe are the bounds
which

which nature dictates for the year, but what could dictate the modern French Calendar, is difficult to fay—it differs from the old Almanack in every refpect for the worfe.

Authors

Authors improperly paired.

THERE is fcarcely a great genius in any country that has not a refemblance found for him in another.

Thus Moliere is the Terence of France —Spencer is the Ariofto, and Milton the Taffo of England—Prior and La Fontaine are affociated—and Corneille is placed by his countrymen in the fame clafs as Shakefpeare.

Moliere and Terence poffefs nothing in common, but each having written comedies—they differ in genius, in ftyle, and in every other refpect. Spencer and Ariofto are lefs unlike, but Milton and Taffo vary in every point, except employing their genius in epic poetry.

Prior

Prior and La Fontaine tell ftories with equal grace, * but the latter has told moft. Shakefpeare and Corneille, it is true, writ many plays, which circumftance is all that they have in common.

Paffages may be extracted to fhew a refemblance of authors; but as a diffimilitude cannot be proved by the fame means, I would requeft the reader's attention to the following letter of Corneille to St. Evremond, and let him endeavour, by the utmoft effort of his imagination, to conceive it written by one who

* Thefe lines were written on a blank leaf of Prior.

Mat Prior (to me 'tis exceedingly plain)
Deferves to be reckoned the Englifh Fontaine,
And Monfieur la Fontaine can never go higher
Than praife to obtain as the French Matthew Prior.
    Thus when Elizabeth defir'd
That Melville would acknowledge fairly,
    Whether herfelf he moft admired,
Or his own Sovere'gn Lady Mary,
The puzzled Knight his anfwer thus expreff'd:
In her own country, *each* is handfomeft.

who could poffibly be the fame in any country, that Shakefpeare is in England.

" Vous m'honorez de vôtre eftime en
" un tems où il femble qu'il y ait un
" parti fait pour ne m'en laiffer aucune.
" Vous me confolez glorìeufement de la
" délicateffe de nôtre Siecle, quand vous
" daïgnez m'attribuer le bon goût de
" l'antiquitè. Je vous avoüie après cela,
" que je penfe avoir quelque droit de
" traiter de ridicules ces vains trophèes
" qu' on établit fur le débris imaginaire
" des miens : et de regarder avec pitié
" ces opiniâtres entêtemens qu' on avoit
" pour les anciens Héros refondus a nôtre
" mode."

'If Corneille muft have a counterpart in England, I fhould rather feek it in Rowe than Shakefpeare.

In fact they did not live in the fame ftate of fociety—France was advancing

in

in refinement and tafte when Corneille
lived, but neither one nor the other exifted in England in the days of Shakefpeare. This circumftance alone would
be a prefumption againft their being in
the fame clafs of writers.

The Cup-bearer. An Indian Tale.

BEFORE the contention of Schâh Jehan's four fons to determine who fhould poffefs the throne of their father, Indoftan was in perfect peace and tranquillity. The empire was not then divided into contending parties, mutually feeking each other's deftruction, but the great officers of the court fought health and amufement by hunting the beafts of the foreft.

Jeffom, Emir al Omrah, Cup-bearer to the Schâh, one day purfuing a fwift Nyl-gau, it led him to the mountains adjacent to Dehli, where the creature eluded the dogs and the hunters. The Emir difmounting from his horfe, and winding his way between the rocks, at laft fat down under the fhade of a fpreading platanus.

tanus. Nature exhaufted by fatigue was recruiting herfelf by fleep—moments of infenfibility, yet delicious on reflection. Awaking, he found before him an old man wrapped in a fhawl, who, after his Salam, exprefled a fear that he had unintentionally difturbed his repofe, and afked whether he chofe any refrefhment? A draught of water would be pleafant to me faid the Cup-bearer. The other retired, but foon returned with a bowl filled with the pureft element, and cool as the rock from whence it iflued. As the Emir took it in his hand; "Stay," fays the old-man, adding three drops from a chryftal veflel. After the Emir had drank, he required the meaning of the addition? "The water was drink," faid the other, "but the drops were medicine. You have fatigued yourfelf by the chace, and fomething was wanting to reftore the ftrength you had loft by exercife." "Strength *loft* by exercife!" exclaimed the Emir, "I exercife myfelf to *procure*, not to *lofe*

ftrength."

ſtrength." "How ſtrength is to be acquired by fatigue, I am yet to learn,"
replied the old-man; the human machine, like every other, wears out by
friction, and it is preſerved by reſt."
"I thought," returned the other, "that
all men were agreed in the uſe, and indeed, neceſſity of exerciſe." Not all,"
replied the old man; our "neighbours,
the Perſians, are not fond of unneceſſary
motion, and their neighbours, the Turks,
have a proverb, That it is better to ride,
than to walk—to ſit, than to ſtand—and
that death is the beſt of all. The Franguis, indeed, who of late have forced
themſelves into this country, have that
reſtleſſneſs which you conſider as eſſential
to health. Where there is intemperance,
exerciſe may be neceſſary; and hard labour requires additional nouriſhment;
but the eaſy office of Cup-bearer to the
Schâh (for ſo your robe declares you)
requires not the labour of exerciſe to

counteract

counteract any ill effects arising from your high ſtation."

The Emir did not altohether agree to this, but before he could reply, a peaſant addreſſed the old-man, complaining of tormenting pains in his ſtomach, and begged his aſſiſtance. " Friend," ſays the doctor, " addreſs thyſelf, through the prophet, to the great diſpoſer of health; I can do nothing without ſuperior aſſiſtance—but this is thy *earthly* remedy— drop thrice from this ſmall vial into a large draught of water, and eat nothing until to-morrow. Remember—three drops, and no more."

He was ſcarce gone when another patient came with a different complaint; but the preſcription was the ſame.

The Emir wanted not curioſity, but finding himſelf ſufficiently refreſhed, withheld farther enquiry—thanked the

doctor,

doctor, for so he appeared to be, and departed.

When Schâh Jehan drank; to do his Cup-bearer honour, he always prefented him with the remainder of his draught, which the Emir took, offering up a prayer to the prophet for the Emperor's welfare.

The Schâh loved wine, and could bear much without intoxication : the Emir being of a contrary temperament, it frequently happened that he had more cups to finifh than were confiftent with that clearnefs of underftanding that fhould accompany an addrefs to the holy prophet. In confequence, large pimples began to cover his nofe, his legs fwelled, his beard became fcanty, and the ladies of the Haram complained that his breath was offenfive. The court phyficians were called in, who prefcribed all the coftly medicines of the eaft; but to no purpofe.

The

The fymptoms growing worfe and worfe, by mere chance the Emir recol-lected the old-man of the mountain. Too weak to fit on horfeback, he was conveyed to him in a litter. "When I was here before," faid the Emir, "I was your gueft, permit me now to be your patient." "Willingly," faid the other, "put three drops from this vial into a veffel of water, drink it, and nothing elfe, for the reft of the day." "Impoffible," replied the other, "I muft often take the cup of honour from the hand of my bountiful mafter." "Then," pronounced the phyfician, "you will take the cup of death—the leaft particle of heterogeneous mixture with my medicine inftantly becomes fatal!"

As the Schâh loved the Emir better than his other attendant flaves, he permitted the favourite to be abfent for a feafon; conceiving that the talifman of the fage (for fuch he thought the doc-

B b 3   tor's

tor's three drops to be) required the prefence of the patient.

The doctor continuing the fame prefcription, and the patient his prompt obedience; many days had not elapfed, before the health of the Emir was in all refpects much improved. The carbuncles had left his nofe, his beard increafed, his legs decreafed, and his breath no longer poifoned the atmofphere. " Yet, " a little while," faid the learned phyfician, " and the angel of health may deign to take up his abode with you, and difmifs the angel of death to fearch for other victims."

Many people came from the adjacent country feeking the doctor's advice, which was always given in the fame words, with the fame medicine; and with fuch great fuccefs, that the phyficians of the province loft their reputation and practice.

" Of

" Of what can thefe precious drops confift?" revolved the Emir, equally ad-miring the fimplicity and efficacy of the prefcription. Tho' unable to penetrate the myftery, yet finding that he was quite recovered, and longing to prefent him-felf to his mafter, and indeed to his mif-treffes, he took a grateful leave of the doctor, who, refufing all reward, difmiffed his patient by faying—" My medicine (under the power in whofe hands are health and ficknefs) has performed its accuftomed effects; but as fome time muft elapfe before the narrow pores of the fkin can difcharge what yet remains of it in your conftitution, the cup of ho-nour muft be refufed, unlefs you wifh to make another vifit to your doctor.

A horfe richly caparifoned carried the Emir to Dehli, attended by troops of fervants rejoicing in his health.

B b 4　　　　When

When he kiffed the ground before the feet of Schâh Jehan, he was at firft received as one unknown; the efficacious medicine having made him a new man.

"A cup of wine!" faid the Schâh, "let the great phyfician know, who it is that wifhes him a long enjoyment for himfelf of the bleffing he procures for others. Give him a robe of honour, and let me fee and reward the fage who poffeffes the fource of health!" Two meffengers departed with fpeed to carry the words and robe to the old man of the mountain.

When the Schâh had drank, he gracioufly prefented the remaining wine to his reftored Cup-bearer; who, taking the veffel, attempted thrice to bear it to his lips—but in vain! the doctor's injunction at parting being ftill frefh in his remembrance—and, not to drink, was lofs of his high office; perhaps, of life.

The

The Schâh perceiving that his cup was rejected, gave way to wrath—" Take that flave from my prefence," he exclaimed, and as he refufes *wine* from the hand of his mafter, let *water* be his only beverage—Begone !"

The meffengers to the mountain were not long in fpeeding acrofs the plain of Dehli; they haftily invefted the doctor with his Kalaat, and brought him into the prefence of the Emperor. " Approach," faid the Schâh, " relate by what good fortune thou art poffeffed of that grand elixir which the fages of the eaft and weft have been fo long endeavouring to obtain." " Thy flave," replied the doctor, " has no fuch poffeffion." " Is it a talifman, then?" faid the Schâh—" Nor talifman have I," continued the old man; " If thou commandeft me to difclofe my fecret—thy flave muft obey—but, once difclofed, the virtue of the medicine ceafes." " Thou doft but more and

more

more inflame my curiofity," uttered the Schâh with impatience—" It becomes my duty to gratify it," humbly replied the doctor—" In my early youth I remarked the effects of imagination on the human mind—nothing is too ftrange for the imagination to conceive, and no effect too great for it to produce—by imagination we almoft become the thing we wifh to be. This difcovery is open to all, and all may make the fame ufe of it as myfelf. Much later in life I difcovered intemperance to be the origin of difeafe, and the haftener of death. Of this truth experience only brings a belief, we having long fixed habit, the appetite for pleafure, and prejudice, to oppofe and vanquifh. As the works of nature are all-perfect, it is by acting contrary to her laws that we induce imperfection and difeafe; and nothing but the propenfity of nature to recover, and reft in the centre from which we have forced her, can ever reftore us to our priftine perfection and health. If
there

there are medicines which can affift this
propenfity, let us ufe them; but how
can we be certain that we do not retard,
inftead of affift, operations, the caufes of
which are beyond our weak intellects t
invefligate ?"

" But, the Three drops"—interrupted
the Schâh; (for all fovereigns hate information, tho' they afk it, and fcarcely
admit a reply to their own queftions.)

" Thefe," anfwered the doctor, " come
under the head of imagination."—

" Tell me the fecret of the Three
drops," faid the Schâh, (beginning to
lofe his temper) " and keep all the reft
to yourfelf."

" I was haftening to convince the Emperor," meekly replied the old-man,
" that I poffefs neither medical fecret nor
talifman

talifman—but thy flave ceafes to fpeak, as
his words find no favour before thee"—

" Proceed," faid the Schâh—

" When a patient comes to me," continued the doctor, " I confider him as
having fuffered, by forcing nature from
her feat. If we knew what would reftore her firft pofition, or knowing the
medicine how to make the application, it would be well—but as we do
not, I leave the work to her own powerful efforts. Intemperance being moft
probably the caufe of the diforder, abftinence is moft likely to be the cure. But
this is too fimple a remedy: there muft
be fomething to act on the imagination.
My Three drops do this office, which are
the fame fluid as that which receives
them—*water*—but they have an air of
myftery, and appear in the form of a powerful medicine, whofe quantity muft not
be miftaken. To prevent my patient re-
lapfing

lapſing into the intemperance which produced his complaint, and muſt retard his
cure; I enjoin ſtrict abſtinence, that the
effect of the medicine may not be coun-
teracted. But the whole, means no more,
than removing the effect by deſtroying
the cauſe, and leaving nature at liberty
to do a work which cannot ſafely be
truſted in other hands."

" What !" ſays the Schâh, with contempt, " are thy ſo-much-famed Three
drops, nothing but water?"

" If they have fame," reſpectfully replied the doctor, " let us ſuppoſe they
deſerve it—I told you, Sir, that the diſ-
covery once made, my art was at an
 ̄ end."—

" So," ſaid the Schâh, with apparent
good-humour, " inſtead of puniſhing the
Cup-bearer, I have been his phyſician,
and ordered him the invaluable medicine
of

of the Three drops! Bring him again to my prefence, and it fhall not be my fault if ever again he has occafion to vifit the old man of the mountain."

On Beauty,

MUCH has been written upon the principle of beautiful forms, but nothing seems to have been determined, unlefs for *European* Beauty. If the Afiatic artifts have treated this fubject, their principle, as we may judge from their tafte and practice, muft be very different from ours; whence we may conclude that there is no principle of *general* Beauty, but as Prior fays,

    " 'Tis refted in the Lover's fancy."

This confideration fhould not prevent us from ftudying our own principle of beautiful forms, as it is the foundation of the ornamental part of fculpture, painting, and architecture, and of the proportion and features of the human figure.

We

We feem to have implicitly adopted Grecian ideas, from whence we may account for the prevalence of the antique profile in modern pictures; by which, if the fubjects are from our own hiftory, we have the incoherent mixture of ancient faces expreffing modern characters, and Greeks performing the parts of Englishmen. But from whence did the Greeks take their ftraight profile? Not from nature, for it has every appearance of artifice, although it exifts in a few faces which muft poffefs other qualifications to be thought beautiful. Profeffor Camper, in his Book upon the different Forms of the Human Cranium, feems to have traced this ftyle of face to its fource.*

The projection of the mouth and flat nofe marks that kind of face which is neareft allied to brutality. There is but

one

---

* In what follows, his ideas and mine are fo blended, that I cannot pretend to feparate them.

one degree between a dog—monkey—
ape—ouran-outang—kalmuc and negro.
From the laft to the European face are
many degrees,* which might be fupplied by a general acquaintance with the
human

* The time feems approaching when the European and African face will be more nearly of the
fame character; and the European and Indian features are alfo blending apace. There is fcarce a
fchool for either fex in the kingdom, in which are
not to be found many children of the mixed race
belonging to opulent fathers—fome of thefe are
born to great fortunes, or may naturally expect
them: they marry with perfons of this country, and
communicate their fhape and colour to their future
families; by degrees, perfectly deftroying the Englifh
form, feature, and complexion, which have been
the envy and admiration of the European world.
Perhaps the Spanifh phrafe of " Old Chriftian," to
diftinguifh a perfon not fprung from Moorifh connections, may have in this country fome equivalent to exprefs a family untainted with African or
Indian mixture. I mean no difrefpect to my fable
brethren, but as we were intended by nature to be
feparate, I am forry that commerce has been the
means of uniting us to our mutual difadvantage.

C c

human fpecies—between the beft modern faces and the antique are ftill many gradations.

It is highly probable that the Greeks obferved the near refemblance between the loweft clafs of human faces and monkeys, and, in confequence, conceived Beauty to be far removed from it. As the lower part of the brutal face projected, the human face fublime fhould be depreffed in that part; and, as in the former there was a defcent from the forehead to the nofe, in the latter it fhould be perpendicular.‡ As a fmall fpace between the eyes refembles an ape, therefore, to look like a man, they made the diftance wide. As a great breadth of cranium at the eyes ending above in a narrow forehead, and below in a peaked chin, marked the face of a favage, the Greeks

‡ Nor was this always thought fufficient, for to remove as far as poffible from the projecting mouth, the head (as in the Antinous) is made to recline.

Greeks gave a fquarenefs of forehead, and breadth of face below, to exprefs dignity of character.

Thefe principles clearly account for the Grecian face; but as all extravagance is bad, the antique caft of features, to impartial eyes, is not the moft beautiful, becaufe it is beyond the mark.

An

An Odd Character.

WHEN we are at peace with the world, and the world is at peace with us, the fummer ramblers of England vifit the Continent, and go through France to Switzerland; where, without any relifh of the peculiar circumftances of the country, they fpend their time moft dolefully. At their return, they triumph over the ignorance of thofe who never ftrayed from home, and affure them of the infinite pleafure they have had from their tour.

But when war confines us within our own ifland, we go as far as we can; that is, to the fea-coaft, which muft ferve inftead of going farther.

All

All well-frequented watering places offer to the attentive obferver a great variety of characters, more or lefs amufing. Some few really come for health, more for pleafure, but with moft the motive is idlenefs—perfons to whom not only the day, but every hour is much too long—perfons, as Ranger in the play exprefles it, " who had rather go to the Devil than ftay at home." Sometimes we meet with an agreeable exception, and fometimes with an oddity.

A week's refidence at Weymouth gave me an opportunity of converfing with a fingular character. We had often met—at the coffee-houfe—at the library, and had made fome little progrefs towards an acquaintance; when, without any provocation on my part, he feemed rather to fhun, than to feek me. However, we were accidentally imprifoned in the Camera-Obfcura, and could not well avoid going down the hill in company together,

C c 3   when

when he expreſſed himſelf nearly in this
manner. " I am afraid you think me
ſomething worſe than an odd fellow."—
To which, receiving no reply—he continued—" I confeſs the apparent abſurdity
of my way of life. It is upon a principle
which differs ſo much from common
cuſtom, that it lies perfectly open to attacks which I ſhall not even attempt to
repel—I am content to be thought incapable of defending myſelf, and if non-
reſiſtance in one party can communicate
any honour to the other, my adverſary
may enjoy all the triumph of ſuch a victory—my ſyſtem is my own, and made
for myſelf alone.

" In my early days I was not long in
obſerving, that by far the greateſt part of
life's troubles were not upon our own account; but that of others—that it was in
the power of one perſon to make a hundred miſerable, by their partaking of his
perſonal afflictions; but that he could
make

make but one happy, by partaking of his perfonal pleafures—this is undoubtedly a lofing trade, but yet this is the commerce of fociety. A man of a philanthropic temper becomes acquainted with thofe about him; his acquaintance with fome produces friendfhip, and his friendfhips produce forrow. Every trouble of mind, or difeafe, of your friends, affects you: it is true you alfo participate their pleafures, as far as they can be communicated; but thefe are not in equal proportions.

" Should your friend increafe his poffeffions, you are not the richer; but if he is in want, you are the poorer—if he be in health, as it is a thing in courfe, you do not rejoice; but if he is fick, you mourn—if he poffeffes an agreeable wife, you have none of his pleafure; but if he lofes her, his pain is poured into your bofom.

Suppofe

" Suppofe life paffes without any exertions of friendfhip, but merely in a belief,
that if they were required they would be
made—I then fee my friend advance in
years—he lofes his perfon and ftrength
by degrees—death fets his mark upon
him, and at laft claims him for his own.
What I fee in him, he fees in me; and
all thofe fenfations are multiplied according to the number of our intimate connections.

" Fully fenfible of this truth, I very early
in life determined to have no friend at all.
To accomplifh this intention, my plan
has been to fhift my refidence from place
to place ; to have many acquaintance, but
no friends. The common fcenes of public
amufement I vifit occafionally, and fometimes bury myfelf in London. If I wifh
to improve, I retire ; if to amufe myfelf,
I join in fuch accidental parties as occur,
and like the butterfly, play among the
flowers, but fix on none. If an acquaintance

quaintance with an agreeable perfon improves too faft, and I begin to feel something like an attachment, I take it as a hint for shifting my quarters, and decamp before the fetter is faftened. To confefs the truth, I more than fufpect that I have been too long acquainted with you: I fhall quit this place immediately, left to-morrow I fhould feel myfelf your friend."

He then redoubled his pace, as if willing to avoid my reply. I indulged him in his wifh, and was not forry to be excufed from continuing a converfation I could not fupport with any other than common arguments; which feldom have any effect upon thofe who fo boldly differ from principles long eftablifhed, and fuppofed to be true.

Something

Something beyond us, neceſſary.

" I COULD move this globe, ſaid Archimedes, if I had another whereon to
fix my lever." Hume ſhrewdly obferves, that prieſts having found, what
Archimedes wanted, another world to
reſt on, it is no wonder they move this
at their pleaſure.

In all purſuits, whether of the artiſt,
moraliſt, or the divine, it is neceſſary to
have ſomething *beyond ourſelves* on which
we are to fix; or elſe, to uſe the above
figure, our machinery is of no effect.

A painter has, or ought to have, ſomething in his imagination beyond the immediate objects of his attention. The
moraliſt ſearches for the *perfect good*, and
the

the religionift directs all his hopes to a
life hereafter.

If we could demonftrate to the artift,
the moral philofopher, and the chriftian,
that they are in purfuit of a fhadow—that
there is no *beau ideal*—no *perfect good*—
and that this life is the " Be-all and End-
all," we fhould do thefe people irrepa-
rable damage—for this world can never
be moved, unlefs there is another whereon
to fix the lever.

Should it be afked, What are thofe
points of perfection to which man afpires?
It may be anfwered, That, perhaps, they
do not exift at all.   But as fuch a reply
would difcourage a meritorious purfuit,
let us rather fay, that great effects are not
produced by exact definitions, or by perfectly knowing the things to which we
afpire.   The fublime is always painted
by a broad pencil.   The poet who de-
                                    fcribes

fcribes minutely, is not great—diftinct defcription is for inferior purpofes.

" I faw a fmith ftand on his hammer, thus—
With open mouth fwallowing a taylor's news."

The expreffion for the fubject is admirable, but no one would call it fublime.

When Milton, in his Defcription of Satan, fays that

" On his creft fat horror plum'd"—

No particular idea is prefented, for what is the form of horror? Juft what your imagination chufes to make it—fome terrible thing, but what, we know not; and becaufe we know it not, our ideas expand until we create a grand, tho' indiftinct image, and feel its fublimity. The height of a mountain envelloped with clouds, rifes upon the imagination, becaufe its top is concealed.

This

This principle is equally efficacious on religious fubjects.

When we are told in general terms that the future life is to be happy or miferable beyond conception; there is fomething placed out of our reach, which is the ideal point—but if we defcend to particulars, and figure, as we fee in pictures of the Laft Judgement, Angels playing on harps, and Devils brandifhing pitch-forks; not even Michael Angelo's genius could prevent the fubject from being ridiculous. Perhaps it is the effect of this principle that induces me to think meanly of the ceremonies of the Roman Church, which appear to me minute, and particular—therefore not fublime.

It has been juftly remarked, that the French, by confidering Popery and Chriftianity as the fame, have made the latter fuffer for the faults of the former. The late

late revolution feems to have taken from the French in every refpect " the other world on which to fix the lever." Their exhibition of a real woman to be wor-fhipped under the character of the God-defs of Liberty, is lefs ideal than when, in their Popifh days, they reprefented the Deity under a corporeal form—in both they offended true tafte as much as true religion, for from the above principle the object of our devotion fhould not be feen, but conceived.

By the deftruction of royalty there is no court from which we are to take the *beau ideal* of politenefs. That of France had been long in poffeffion of the privi-lege of fetting fafhions for the reft of Europe. Even the London newfpapers (notwithftanding the brilliancy of our own court) once a month at leaft, gave us a detail of the modes of Paris; but fince there has been no King or Queen to confider as the points above us, they

fee

fee the abfurdity of taking a fafhion from Citizens* —— or their wives. Thefe auguft perfonages, though followed by all the Mother Red-caps in the Republic, can hardly be offered as models to be copied by the Dukes and Ducheffes of England.

By fixing the attention of the people upon the mean vulgar tunes of Ça ira, and the Carmagnole March,‡ there is an

end

* When this effay was written, the names of two perfons were inferted, who foon after loft their heads—two others were added, who met with the fame fate—I will mention no more, but leave it to the reader to fill up the blanks with " the poor players of the prefent hour," as they pafs in fucceffion.

‡ Major Tench, in the account of his imprifonment in France, has the following paffages:—" I went upon Eafter Sunday to the Cathedral—in the moft folemn part of the fervice, the Marfeillois Hymn was heard from the organ : that war-whoop to whofe found the bands of regicides who attacked their fovereign in his palace marched ; and which, during the laft three years, has been the watchword

end of all attempts to the musical sublime.† Poetry is degenerated into jaco-
bine ballads; and painting, having lost
its grand and religious subjects, does not
aspire beyond the death of a Marat or
Pelletier.

By

word of violence, rapine, and murder. I was once
carelessly humming at the fire-side the Carmagnole,
when a Lady suddenly interrupting me, exclaimed
—" For God's sake cease that hateful tune! It
brings to my remembrance nothing but massacres
and guillotines." Again—" The national taste has
suffered equal degradation. The Dramas of Racine,
and the Odes and Epistles of Boileau, are supplanted
by crude declamatory productions, to which the
revolutionary spirit has given birth."

† We may pronounce, from experience, on the
effect of having our ears dinned by the eternal repetition of some popular tune, which is to super-
cede all other music, let its merit be ever so great.
Formerly the musical performances at the Theatres
were interrupted by *Roast-beef*. Of late, *Roast-beef*
has been abandoned, and given place to that de-
vout and delectable canticle *God save the King*;
which we must sing over and over again, by way
of a loyal English reply to French Republican dit-
ties. Would that France were a Monarchy again!

By their abolition of Chriftianity (whatever opinion they may entertain of its truth) one great fource of the fublime in mufic, painting, morality, and religion, is utterly deftroyed.

For the reft of the world it is a melancholy confideration, that the ftudies of fo great and enlightened a country as France fhould be wrongly directed. This unfortunate circumftance may tend to the deftruction of thofe arts and fciences which have coft us fo much trouble and ftudy to acquire.

When the above obfervations were made, the French in two years had become in manners a new people, and altered, in moft refpects, very much for the worfe: perhaps, before thefe remarks will be read, another alteration may take
place

D d

place*—it will give the writer much pleafure if every circumftance he has mentioned may accord only with the prefent moment.

* " En tems d'orage, le Ciel change á tout moment: et le tableau, qu'on en a fait, n'a été vrai, qu'un inftant."

Influence of Appellations.

" WHAT is there in a name," fays Juliet, " that which we call a rofe, by any other name would fmell as fweet." No doubt, if the rofe had not that appellation, its fweetnefs would fpeak for itfelf; but if diftinguifhed by a word to which we had previoufly attached fome difagreeable meaning, the affociation of ideas might produce a fenfation to the difadvantage even of this lovely flower.

Montaigne, and Sterne (his imitator) think that a man's fuccefs in life may depend on his name; which is not altogether fo fanciful—how many owe their fortune to their being called after a godfather?

There

There are some instances of our continuing in a constant state of misconduct, from a misapplication of names, or by applying the usual meaning of a term to a purpose with which it is totally disconnected. Thus, when Boniface is told, " that his ale is confounded strong," he replies, " how else should we be strong that drink it?" When the common people are depressed, they take a dram because it is called spirit; they then conceive they have got what they wanted, and must of course be merry. Had it not been for the unfortunate epithet of *strong*, applied to beer, and the term *spirit* being given to brandy, people would never have guessed that ale gave them strength, or brandy created spirits. It is an unfortunate circumstance that brandy is called also aqua-vitæ, and eau-de-vie, by which it has proved to nations, who never heard of the English term, *spirit*, to be aqua-mortis and eau-de-mort. This liquid having a name so contrary to its

real

real effect, has been, and will continue to be, the caufe of more deftruction than the fword or the peftilence.

The common diforder, a cold, by being fo named, has been the death of thoufands—being called a *cold*, people conceive it fhould be oppofed by *heat*, and heat muft neceffarily expel cold. By acting upon this principle, a flight fever becomes dangerous, and what the ufual efforts of nature would have cured in a few days, is now changed to a diforder frequently beyond the reach of medicine.

The *word* Tax is deteftable, although the *thing* be unavoidable; it is therefore prudent in a minifter to prevent (if poffible) its being ever pronounced. He does prevent it, by concealing the tax in the price of the commodity inftead of keeping it diftinct—Thus, if we buy a pair of fhoes, and the tax is included in the coft, we only buy the fhoes dear, we

D d 3   do

do not pay a tax; but if we gave half the price for the ſhoes, and paid, ſeparately, a tax, the fifth part of that included in the ſhoes, the burthen would be thought intolerable. A two-ſhilling ſtamp being ſeparated from the price of the hat, is a tax that is felt; but the five-ſhilling tax included in the ſhoes is unnoticed. We are content to buy dear, but much dif-pleaſed at being taxed—let the roſe have its perfume, but call it by another name.

The word *exciſe* is rather worſe than *tax*, and an exciſeman the worſt of all tax-gatherers. The late Duke of Bed-ford had nearly loſt his life at Exeter, by ſimply giving his vote for making a commodity ſubject to the exciſe—had it been only taxed, he might have paſſed to Taviſtoke unmoleſted.

When the people of Europe firſt began to cultivate the lands in the Weſt-Indies, they ſoon experienced that the climate

was

was too hot for hard work—they had re-
courfe to Africa for labourers, in which
they did no more on the weftern coaft,
than had been done in the eaftern part of
that vaft continent, from the earlieft antiquity. The flave-trade on the fhore
of the Red-fea, as Bruce informs us, takes
off thoufands of negroes for Arabia, Perfia, and India; fo that the inhabitants of
Africa feem to be doomed to labour, that
the reft of the world may live in luxury.

In thofe days of philanthropy, when
prifons muft be palaces, when the rich
muft be poor, the poor rich, and all men
and things reduced to a happy equality—
who can bear the thought of eating the
produce of a plant which is watered with
the tears and blood of its miferable cultivators? This might be made a moft pathetic picture, but does it not owe all its
effect to the word *flave*? Suppofe at firft
the planters had called thefe labourers
black fervants, would any perfon have

objected

objected to their being brought from Africa, (where, in fact, they are in the moft vile of all fituations) and exalted from flaves to fervants ?

My intention is not to enter upon a fubject which has of late employed fo many writers, but merely to fhew the effect of a *word* independently of the *thing* to which it is applied.

No army or navy can poffibly exift without fubordination or difcipline—but, if living under an abfolute government conftitutes flavery, what flaves are more compleatly fo than foldiers and failors ?* However, as the difgraceful term is not beftowed on them, they feel that they are in the full enjoyment of all the rights and privileges of free-born Englifhmen.

A

* This being written many years fince, ought not to be applied to late events.

A mifnomer, we fee, is of confequence
in the common affairs of life, as well as
in law, with, this difference to its difadvantage, that it cannot fo eafily be corrected; but we muft fubmit to its effects,
without hope of redrefs, until fomething
fhall be found fufficient to fubdue the
force of cuftom long-eftablifhed.

On Executions.

" MY betters are worfe than me," fays Betty in Jofeph Andrews. To adopt the fame paradoxical ftyle, it may be faid, that fome of our improvements are for our difadvantage.

Mr. Howard has been the occafion of many alterations for the worfe, under an idea of remedying grievances upon philanthropic principles.

When a man by committing a crime has incurred the penalty of the law, it is neceffary that he fhould be kept in fafe cuftody until he is tried or punifhed— but if his prifon be a large magnificent building (notwithftanding the mifery of the cells) he confiders himfelf as a Being

of

of confequence—moft probably the grandeur of the place takes from him all humiliating thoughts which lead to repentance.

If I have fome objections to our improvements of prifons, I have more to the improvements in the mode of executions.

Formerly, a culprit walked to the gallows, where he fpent an hour in praying and finging a penitential pfalm (which produces a great effect upon the fpectators) after which, he was thrown off a ladder, and left hanging, according to the vulgar phrafe, like a dog.

The firft improvement was conveying condemned prifoners in a cart—this leffened the ignominy of the execution, but encreafed the horror of the previous circumftances, as a cart is an ignoble carriage, and the perfons of the criminals

were

were more expofed, and marked out as objects of attention—but it had one bad confequence—the cart (by thofe who could pay for it) was frequently changed for a coach—and to ride in a coach is a defirable thing in the idea of the common people. .

The place of execution for London was once two miles out of town—by degrees, the houfes reached it, and the people who lived in them not relifhing fuch exhibitions as well as the common people, got the place changed for the prifon door —this brought on the dropping platform. The effect of executions, as examples, is much diminifhed by thefe improvements. The long proceffion and difgraceful expofure are loft, and inftead of being " hanged like a dog," as was once the cafe, it is now dying like a gentleman.

Let me digrefs a moment from my prefent fubject, to cenfure the mode of
executions

executions in Italy and Spain, as I find it related in books of travels. In Rome, when a man is hanged, the executioner fits upon his fhoulders—in Spain he does the fame, with the addition (as I am informed) of running into the criminal's body long fpurs, which he wears at his heels. This does not produce the effect of a criminal fuffering the penalty of the law, but of a man murdered in public for the entertainment of the rabble, efpecially when they add to it the twirling round of the body, as is the cuftom in fome places.

Perhaps there are few natural deaths but are more painful than hanging—no one would wifh to add to its pains whatever they are, but it is furely unwife to take from the apparatus that which adds fo much to the effect produced upon the fpectators. Thefe reflections were occafioned by the following incident.

Two

Two robbers had been taken up in the country—confined in the county gaol (before Mr. Howard's improvements)—tried, and condemned to be hanged. Some circumſtance occurred on their trial which made it neceſſary for a turnkey of Newgate to viſit them in the country priſon. He was aſked, " How he found them, and what was their behaviour?" " As low as the Devil," he replied, " but there is no one can blame them—they don't like being in a ſhabby country priſon—if they were with us in Newgate, and were to be hanged at our Drop, I'd be d—d if they'd care a farthing."

A

A proper Length neceſſary for Muſical and Literary Productions.

ALL productions of art which cannot, like painting and ſtatuary, produce an inſtant effect, ought to be of that duration as neither to fatigue the attention by length, nor prevent the neceſſary impreſſion on the mind for want of it.

If this principle had ever been fixed as neceſſary to produce effect, ſo many compoſitions in muſic and literature would not have failed in giving that pleaſure to the ſenſe or imagination, which their excellence muſt otherwiſe have commanded. But ſo far from any ſuch principle being fixed, it does not ſeem to have occurred that there is any reaſon for its exiſtence.

If

If the Iliad had not been longer than one of its books, it would certainly have been too fhort; and there are few perfons, if they would be honeft, but feel twenty-four books much too long. Virgil, fays Addifon, by comprizing his Poem in twelve books, pretended but to half the merit of the Iliad. What his pretenfions were cannot now be known, but if his plan were compleated in the prefent length of the Æneid, it muft have diminifhed its effect to have made it longer.

The Oratorio of Judas Maccabæus poffeffes fome of the fineft fpecimens of Handel's compofitions. The fong "*Father of Heaven*" has no other fault than being a little too long. I remember it encored twice, and a third encore attempted. The effect of this repetition, on my fenfations, was exceedingly diftrefsful, and produced a mental furfeit, which, like that of the ftomach, took much time to remove.

All

All German compofers have too many movements in their fymphonies, and make their movements too long. Croft's Anthems merit the fame cenfure. Each act of an Opera or Oratorio, is at leaft one third too long. Any fong, except the old ballad (where the fame air is repeated) fhould confift but of three verfes, which, in general, is the beft number. An air, with variations, muft have peculiar merit to admit of more than fix. I once heard a German lutenift play an air of this fort with four and twenty variations, every ftrain of which he moft punctually repeated! In the performances of mufic, long cadences, long fwells, and long fhakes, are moft diftreffing things to the afflicted audience—for afflicted they are, notwithftanding they applaud fo loudly.*

Whoever faw a fet of books of many volumes without a fenfation of difguft?

E e   Tho'

---

* See Obfervations on the State of Mufic in London in 1790.

Tho' I never beheld the "dreadful front"
of De Lyra, yet I have feen fo many
others in great libraries, as to make one
cry out with the Hoft in Jofeph Andrews, "What can they all be about?"

If the noble author of the reign of
Henry the Second had reduced his book,
half, or rather, two thirds, it would ftill
have contained all we wifh to know about
the fubject—and great obligations would
the world have had to Mr. Gibbons, if
the gaudy flowers in his extenfive garden
had never vegetated, for alas! "We
better like a field."

If a preacher were to end with merely
giving his text, or after pronouncing a
few fentences, we fhould think he had
mounted the pulpit for nothing; but
good muft be his doctrine, and great muft
be his powers, if we wifh him to remain
in it the ufual length of a long fermon.

No

No perfon in Parliament, to be heard with pleafure and attention, fhould in fpeaking exceed an hour—he may be affured that a longer fpeech is only liftened to by Jupiter, who, we are told, exerts perpetual watchfulnefs.

Half a minute is very long for a fpeech in company—extend it much farther, the looks of our audience fhew that they think us profing.

I might much encreafe thefe inftances, but they are fufficient to eftablifh my pofition—" That a *due* length is neceffary to produce *good* effect."

Aboulhamed

Aboulhamed and the Brahmin.

ABOULHAMED was the only fon of a wealthy merchant at Ormus, and on his father's death poffeffed all his treafure. Everything that riches could beftow was within his power; but he found that there were fome bleffings which riches could not procure—long-life was not to be purchafed; perhaps, for that very reafon he earneftly wifhed for it.

This idea became ftrongly impreffed upon his mind; it was his laft thought at going to reft, and the firft when he awoke.

When once the fpirits are ftrongly moved, they continue the agitation without a frefh effort; it was not then unnatural

tural that his dreams fhould be fometimes on the fubject which had engaged his waking thoughts. One of thefe dreams appeared to him a revelation in vifion of what he fo earneftly wifhed to obtain— his guardian Angel bade him depart for Benares, where he fhould find in the obfervatory, a Brahmin fitting near the great quadrant, who would inform him how to lengthen life.

His imagination dwelt with fo much pleafure on this injunction, that he conceived it to be repeated, and that to delay his voyage would be criminal. After the ufual time he arrived fafely at Benares, and took the earlieft opportunity of vifiting the obfervatory.

Upon actually finding a Brahmin in the place as he had feen him in his dream, Aboulhamed accofted him with a confidence founded on the hope of the Brahmin being fent there to meet him. " Ve-

nerable

nerable fage," fays he, " need I acquaint
you with the caufe which brought me to
Benares?" " It is needlefs," replied the
Brahmin—" Why doft thou defire long-
life? Is it to perfect thyfelf in know-
lege, or in virtue? Haft thou predicted
fome conjunctions of the planets which
thou defireft to fee accomplifhed—Haft
thou entered upon a courfe of ftudy which
the Angel of Death may prevent thy
finifhing, or commenced works of benevolence which the ufual term of human
life is too fhort for bringing to perfection? Aboulhamed with blufhes confeffed, that he wifhed for long-life folely
to enjoy his riches—" Alas!" faid the
Brahmin, " what enjoyment is there of
life when old-age has deftroyed our appe-
tites and paffions? Thy firft wifh fhould
have been for perpetual youth, and then
the other would have been rational.
Know, ftranger, that before thy heart had
begun to beat, the number of its con-
tractions was determined. No art or
earthly

earthly power can add one to the fum, but it depends on thyfelf whether it fhall ue exhaufted fooner or later. At the beginning of things, when Brahma was appointed to create the human fpecies, he judged that 2,831,718,400* pulfations were the proper number for the duration of a life of feventy years—of thefe 100,800* are daily expended. If inftead of this allowance thou wilt force thy heart to beat twice as many, although thy deftiny be not changed, thou liveft but half thy time. By a life of reafon and temperance the laft ftroke is long delayed, but by wafting thy fpirits in folly and riot the appointed number is quickly accomplifhed. Remove the ballance from the machine with which Europeans meafure time, and the wheels will hurry through their proper revolution of thirty hours in a few feconds. Immenfe fhould thy poffeffions be to af-

E e 4

ford

---

* Brahma made his enumeration on the proportion of feventy ftrokes in a minute.

ford the daily expence of 100,800 of the smallest coin—One day's income is too great to be lost—Of how much more consequence then is this sum if applied to Time, which is invaluable? In the diffipation of worldly treasure the frugality of the future may balance the extravagance of the past; but who can say, " I will take from minutes to-morrow, to compensate those I have lost to-day?"

" Thou desirest long-life—are there not many hours in every day which pass unimproved, unemployed, and even unnoticed? Use these first, before thou demandest more. Be assured that the term which nature has allotted to our existence, is sufficient for all *her* purposes, and for all *ours*, if we employ it properly; but if we waste our time instead of improving it, what right have we to complain of wanting that, of which we already possess more than we use?"

Aboulhamed,

Aboulhamed, making his falam to the Brahmin, departed; and like his fellow mortals, felt all the inferiority of being inftructed, without the benefit of the inftruction; for he ftill continued to wifh for life, and ftill continued to fquander it away.

MERCIER, in his Tableau de Paris, remarks—"" That ancient names without " splendor—difmal, plain ftone coffins— " figures fad and uninterefting, fculp- " tured without tafte or proportion; are " the things which fill our churches. " Genius feems to be abafed under the " dominion of terror, and her trembling " hand can only venture to trace images " difmal and monotonous. Contemplate " the ruins of Herculaneum and Portici; " they carry not the impreffion of fo dark " an imagination."

This remark is worthy of fome confideration.

The

The ruins of Rome firſt gave the moderns a hint for ſtudying Antiquities—nothing could be more laudable—thoſe remains ſhewed the ſtate of the arts in a great empire which had copied them from the pureſt Grecian models. Every building, ſtatue, and coin, became a leſſon from a poliſhed, to a barbarous age; and beſides being an object of curioſity, was of the greateſt uſe, as holding up a point of perfection which we ſhould endeavour to attain.

This ſtudy had not long been in vogue, before *barbarous* Antiquity became an object of attention—and deſervedly ſo, as far as ſatisfying our curioſity, in diſcovering what ideas our forefathers entertained of the arts. But when we conſider Gothic ſubjects as models for approbation or imitation; we loſe all the advantages of acquired taſte, and revert to the days of ignorance.

Dugdale's

Dugdale's Monafticon and his St. Paul's, are ufeful and proper fubjects, with the above reftriction. To Hollar we are much indebted for preferving the old Cathedral of London; but let it not be imagined that becaufe Gothic Antiquity is old, it is, therefore, in a polifhed age* to be accounted beautiful, although it undoubtedly poffeffes its own proper merit.

In the beginning of this century was a rage for Roman Antiquities—moft of our travellers confined their remarks to ruined temples, broken columns, mutilated altars, and obliterated coins—fubjects for ridicule to many—but all thefe had their ufe, and led to the improvement of a country in its progrefs towards perfection.

At this time we feem to exert all our powers in reading infcriptions on broken tombftones belonging to " ancient names
without

* See the Effay on this fubject, p. 95.

without fplendour"—in publifhing mutilated figures " fad and uninterefting,
fculptured without tafte or proportion"—
in feals of forgotten bifhops and abbots,
which offer nothing for imitation or improvement, and are fcarcely objects of
curiofity.

Elegant Antiquity engages our attention from its excellence—Barbarous Antiquity we fhould almoft fear to fee, left
cuftom might make us approve what we
ought to avoid.

On Derivation.

ACCIDENT frequently gives birth to words which in fucceeding times are with difficulty traced to their origin.

The terms Whig and Tory have been derived from fo many different fources, that we may prefume their real origin is unknown. The cant words of the moment, being hafty productions, are moft commonly fhort-lived—but fometimes they get firmer hold, and by degrees gain a fettlement in the language, and become part of it.

The term *club* is of this latter fort—it is not only admitted into our own tongue, but has been adopted in France, and is now extending itfelf to other countries.

It

It is therefore become of fufficient confequence to claim the attention of the
literary herald, and to have its origin
fearched; which I believe may be found
in Rufhworth. Who tells us, that in
1645 " there were *affociations* of people
to prevent themfelves from being plun-
dered by either army, called *club*-men,
from the weapons they carried." Club-
men was, as ufual, foon abbreviated to
club—and the term, from being peculiar,
grew by degrees to be general, and applied to affociations of people which had
not before an appropriated title.

It prefently fpread rapidly, and at the
beginning of this century was firmly eftablifhed in England, and now bids fair
to be one of the moft general terms in
Europe.

On Climate.

* * * " I SET out for Dover. Having
" been accuſtomed to conſider the climate
" of this country as much colder than
" that of France, I was aſtoniſhed at the
" mildneſs of the air, the charming ver-
" dure of the fields, the trees in bloſſom,
" and the ſpring in general in a more for-
" ward ſtate than I had left it in my own
" country."

De Pagès.

If we were to eſtimate the heat and
cold of a country ſimply by its diſtance
from the equator, Mr. Pagès was quite
right in the judgment he had formed of
England—but there are many other circumſtances to be conſidered—

Whether

Whether the country be an ifland or part of the Continent?

Whether it has ridges of high mountains?—and

What is its ftate of cultivation?

If it be an ifland, it is lefs hot in fummer, and lefs cold in winter. Of courfe, vegetation begins fooner, and continues longer—but as the fummer heat is greater on the Continent; fruits, fuch as grapes and figs, &c. will ripen there in the fame latitude, which will not bring them to perfection in an ifland. On the other hand, vegetables for the table will flourifh through the winter in an ifland, which would be deftroyed by froft on the Continent.

If there be ridges of high mountains, fuch as the Alps or Pyrenees, the fnow which remains on them undiffolved thro'

F f   the

the fummer, gives a keennefs to the wind blowing from them, which is not felt in a more level country, and retards the fpring—Now, there are no mountains of this fort in England.

If land be well managed, it pufhes forth vegetation fooner and ftronger. The ground in France, it is true, is exten-fively cultivated, but moft miferably ma-nured; nor is the corn-harveft in the north of that country fo forward as in the fouth of England by fome weeks.

One would think thefe truths muft have been long fince difcovered, but they feem to be as much unknown to the ge-neral part of mankind, as if they did not exift.

To this let me add a few extracts from a fenfible, modern traveller, on the cli-mate of Italy—

* * *

* * * " The climate of Naples difap-
" pointed us no lefs. Perpetual rain and
" ftorms, with really cold weather during
" the greater part of our abode there,
" made large fires neceffary, &c."

" The weather at Rome was far from
" uniformly pleafant during our ftay.
" We had much rain, many dull days,
" and fome very cold ones, though no
" fnow. The moft difagreeable and un-
" wholefome circumftance in the climate
" of Italy, is the cold wind that occa-
" fionally blows from the mountains for
" a day or two, often with fuch piercing
" feverity, that no exercife, even in fun-
" fhine, can keep the body warm. * * *

" May 1. Even at this feafon we had
" very cold weather."

" May 2. A moft terribly cold day,
" with much rain, and a violent north-
" eaft wind, &c."

" May

" May 13. The *firſt* thoroughly fine
" day ſince we left Rome."

" May 20. The wind ſo extremely
" cold, that it was impoſſible to enjoy
" anything in the open air."

" May 17. Being Aſcenſion-Day, and
" the painted Madonna having with much
" ado procured very fine weather (for it
" ſeems to be eſteemed a miracle to have
" a fine day at Venice in the middle of
" May) &c."   SMITH.

I could add many more teſtimonies*
to the inclemency of the winters (if that
                                    ſeaſon

---

* Nor indeed are they wanting to prove, that
even the ſummers have at times a daſh of cold,
which one knows not how to think poſſible in a
climate ſo much extolled. The ſenſible and obſerving author of *Lettres d'Italie*, has the following
remark—" Tranſis de froid comme j'aurois crû ne
l'etre jamais en Italie, ni nulle part en cette Saiſon
(19 Juillet) nous avons longè la côte ſous Ville-
franche laiſſant Nice, &c. &c."

feafon may be extended to the end of May) in Italy. A party went from Rome to Naples—refided there a fortnight, in which time not a fingle day occurred that would admit of taking the fmalleft ex-curfion—the weather was a continued courfe of cold wind, rain, fleet, and fnow.

The often-quoted faying of Charles the Second, on the climate of England, is perhaps as true as it is common.

The fouth-coaft of our ifland is natu-rally reforted to by valetudinarians who wifh for a mild air: and although the dif-ference of latitude between Dover and Penzance is not very material, yet the winter is by far moft temperate at the latter of thefe places. This muft arife from other circumftances. There feem to be feveral caufes combined, to produce this effect.

1.

1. When the wind is North, it comes over a large tract of land before it reaches the coast of Dorsetshire, Hampshire, Sussex, and Kent, which is not so with the south-western counties—the eastern coast then from this cause must be colder.

2. The county of Cornwall is surrounded by the sea, except where it joins to Devonshire. The sea being less warm in summer, and less cold in winter, communicates its property to the adjoining land, which is here but of small dimensions, and necessarily partakes of the sea's temperature.

3. As frosts, in general, come with a wind in some point between the north and east; they are found to commence on the Continent before they reach England, and to begin on the north-eastern side of our island before the south-western part is affected: from which cause it happens that many short frosts never reach Devonshire

vonſhire and Cornwall. Suppoſe a froſt
eſtabliſhed in theſe two counties, in common with the reſt of the kingdom—There
will be no thaw until the courſe of the
air be reverſed: as ſoon as the wind
changes to the ſouth-weſt, Cornwall feels
the change firſt, and it is no uncommon
circumſtance to hear of froſt ſtill continuing to the north-eaſt, long after it is
quite gone in that, and the next county.

Theſe cauſes, taken together, clearly
account for the mildneſs of the winter in
the two ſouth-weſtern counties, where,
perhaps, is a more ſteady temperature,
and leſs difference between the extreme
points of heat and cold, than is to be
found in any other part of Europe. As
theſe facts may now be conſidered, from
repeated obſervation, as eſtabliſhed, it is
probable, that a practice begun from neceſſity, may be continued by choice, and
thoſe medical caſes, which require a
milder climate, may be more effectually

relieved

relieved in our own country than any other; especially if the inconveniences (hardships, indeed, to sick persons) be taken into the account, which must unavoidably be endured in foreign countries where the accommodations for travelling, to which we are accustomed, do not exist.

On

On Poetical and Musical Ear.

SOME years ago a controverfy was carried on in a periodical publication upon this queſtion—" Whether there was a neceſſity of a muſical ear for an orator?" Both parties, as uſual, were obſtinate in their reſpective opinions.—Let us examine them.

Thoſe that hold a muſical ear to be neceſſary for an orator, ſupport their opinion in this manner. Every voice has its proper key, from which, though the ſpeaker may wander for the ſake of expreſſion, yet he muſt return to it again— The different modulations of the voice muſt be either a little above, or a little below the key, in which it ſhould always cloſe—Anything out of the key of the

voice

voice offends as much in fpeaking as in finging—Mufic, befides tune, having rhythmus, fo is there a meafure in oratory, which we cannot falfify without offending the ear—As there are refts in mufic, fo there are paufes in fpeaking—from all thefe confiderations, it is evident, that a good ear is equally neceffary for an orator and for a mufician.

To this the other party replies—

As all perfons fpeak, but as all have not a mufical ear, it is evident, that if the latter were neceffary for the well-doing of the former, thofe who have no ear would fpeak in a manner peculiar and difagreeable. If the affertor fay, that it is not in common fpeaking, but in oratory, that a mufical ear is requifite, the other anfwers—That as oratory is but the perfection of fpeaking, there is nothing in oratory that has not its foundation in common fpeech.

But,

But, the fact is, that the tone of the voice in fpeaking, and the tune of the voice in finging, bear not the leaft refemblance to each other—they are formed upon principles directly oppofite*—the different inflections of the voice in fpeaking, are not mufical intervals—in finging, they are, or fhould be, nothing but mufical intervals. If we feel the outfide of the throat while fpeaking, and then change from fpeaking to finging, it will be perceived that the arrangement within which produced fpeaking, muft be changed before we can form a mufical found. Recitative is that fpecies of mufic which bears the neareft refemblance to fpeaking —and fpeaking it is, in mufical founds; but this, as far as tune is concerned, is more removed from common fpeaking, than from finging, becaufe the intervals are tones, femitones, &c.

Pope,

---

* To a perfon of real mufical feeling, there, is nothing more difagreeably diffonant, than the founds occafioned by fpeaking during the performance of mufic.

Pope, though ſo muſical a poet, had
no ear for muſic; the ſame thing is reported of Swift. One of the moſt agreeable ſpeakers I ever knew, had no ear;
and the ſame may be ſaid of ſome of the
firſt orators in both Houſes of Parliament,
but the ſtrongeſt inſtance is found in Garrick—it is an undoubted fact, that he had
no ear. This ſeems to decide the queſtion at once, for it was univerſally allowed that no one ever poſſeſſed the tones
of ſpeaking in a ſuperior degree to this
incomparable actor.

I could much ſtrengthen what has been
advanced by ſome illuſtrious inſtances of
preſent ſtage-performers, and it is to the
diſadvantage of my argument that I muſt
neceſſarily avoid mentioning the names of
perſons ſtill living—my proof muſt therefore reſt on Garrick, in whom could
never be diſcovered any defect of tones
appropriated to the various paſſions, in the

many

many characters he fo fuccefsfully reprefented.

Perhaps, the miftake may have arifen
from ufing the fame terms, in poetry,
oratory, and mufic—as ear, that is, the
difcrimination of intervals, is abfolutely
neceffary in mufic, fo it has alfo been
fuppofed effential to poetry, and oratory
—and this is not the only inftance of
confufion arifing from a wrong application of terms.

On Mental and Corporeal Pleasure.

" I PITY her to my heart," says a lady, when she heard that the husband of her friend was no more, " she will be miserable for the remainder of her life." " She will," replied one of the company (more remarked for his bluntness than discretion) " she will be miserable until her grief has worn itself out, or some superior pain engages her attention."—" Superior pain !" interrupted the lady, " what suffering can be superior to that which we endure from the loss of friends !"—" Our pains are various," replied her antagonist, " whatever we feel at the instant, we think to be the worst possible—he that has the head-ache will never believe the pain in the teeth to be worse—but when the tooth-ache comes, then we exclaim,

" anything

" anything but this I could have borne with patience!" " What are all the aches in nature when compared to the heart-ache? which is what my poor dear friend fuffers!" faid the lady, earneftly. " If you mean by heart-ache," returned the gentleman, " actual bodily pain, I am of opinion that the grief of Mrs. —— will not be of long duration"—" I never heard anything like this," faid the lady, " how can pain of the mind be removed by that of the body? " It is the moft certain way to remove it," faid the other.

The lady not replying, perhaps, from aftonifhment; her opponent bafely took advantage of her filence, to fupport the part he had taken by a much longer fpeech than he ought to have made, had he been contented with his proper fhare of the converfation—

" That the pleafures and pains of the mind (fays he) are fuperior to thofe of the

the body, is one of the falfe maxims which cuftom has fanctified, and which we are taught to believe, in common with other opinions, under the fame authority.

" It can be no falfe maxim to affert, that the fcale which is heavieft, muft preponderate. If we are poffeffing a moderate pleafure, and can enjoy a greater, we naturally quit the former for the latter. If we are enduring pain, and a greater be inflicted, the firft fenfation is done away by the latter. Let us examine corporeal and mental fenfations upon this principle.

" The pleafures of the mind confift in reflection on fuch fubjects, by which it is either inftructed, or entertained. Suppofe it engaged in the moft interefting enquiry in morals, philofophy, or divinity; that it was receiving all the pleafures which the moft favoured author could beftow, or enjoying a creation of its own, and roving at large from one
fancied

fancied blifs to another. All thefe fenfations give place on the fight of a fine
picture, or the hearing of exquifite mufic,
(if we have a feeling of fuch enjoyment,)
or any other delightful appeal to the
fenfes—but they become 'annihilated in
the prefence of a perfon we love—the
pleafures of the mind cannot then be attended to, even in their greateft perfection.

" Let us now fee if bodily pain be not
alfo fuperior to that of the mind.

" Suppofe ourfelves treated with ingra-
titude where obligations have been con-
ferred—that we have parted from friends
for ever—that we have buried our neareft
and deareft connections—" Now, you
come to the point," interrupted the lady.
—" That we are " fteeped in poverty to
the very lips," continued the orator.—
" Let us imagine the heart affailed by any,
or all of thefe torments—in fuch circumftances fhould we attend to a fit of the

G g   colic ?

colic?—No—Of the gout?—The ftone?
—You begin to doubt—I will determine
the point in a moment—let this hot poker
touch you, I warrant all your affliction
vanifhes, and bodily pain is alone trium-
phant.

" To make this the furer, as in the
other cafe, reverfe the propofition. While
your arm is burning, let any one bawl
aloud, that misfortunes are coming on
you thicker than they did upon Job;
you will find that the poker muft be removed, before you can receive the information.

" Now, though we all muft acknowledge the truth of this argument; there
is no one but fears, that to believe it
would be fomething like wickednefs.
" It *is*, it *is* wickednefs," replied the afflicted lady, " and I do not believe a fyllable of all you have faid."

Having

*Having furnished the reader with so
short an answer to the writer's opinions—
let us, for the present, part.*

FINIS.

INDEX.

On